RANDOM
HOUSE
WEBSTER'S
AMERICAN
SIGN
LANGUAGE
COMPUTER
DICTIONARY

RANDOM HOUSE WEBSTER'S
AMERICAN SIGN LANGUAGE
COMPUTER DICTIONARY

Elaine Costello, Ph.D.

Illustrated by
Lois A. Lehman
Linda C. Tom

Random House
New York

Random House Webster's American Sign Language Computer Dictionary

This book is available for special purchases in bulk by organizations and institutions, not for resale, at special discounts. Please direct your inquiries to the Random House Special Sales Department, toll-free 888-591-1200 or fax 212-572-4961.

Please address inquiries about electronic licensing of reference products, for use on a network or in software or on CD-ROM, to the Subsidiary Rights Department, Random House Reference, fax 212-940-7352.

Library of Congress Cataloging-in-Publication Data is available.

Visit the Random House Reference Web site at www.randomwords.com

Typeset and printed in the United States of America.

First Edition
9 8 7 6 5 4 3 2 1
October 2001

ISBN: 0-375-71942-3

New York   Toronto   London   Sydney   Auckland

Contents

Introduction

Why This Dictionary?

New fields bring new concepts into our lives, with new vocabularies that are often obscure and confusing. This has never been more true than now, when the computer revolution that started in the 1980s has made learning its particular lexicon virtually mandatory in schools and in the workplace. *Random House Webster's American Sign Language Computer Dictionary* was compiled in order to fill a real need for a dictionary that standardizes and brings together the terms used every day in the world of computers and those terms as expressed in American Sign Language—the primary language in the world of the Deaf community.

The rapid increase in the use of computers is one of the most significant developments of our time. It has created brand-new ways of communicating and entire new industries. It has, in fact, fashioned a pervasive environment that no one could have imagined a few years ago—a social and economic climate in which everyone who wants to learn to use computers and is given the opportunity to do so can become a productive member of this interlinked electronic universe. The Deaf community is no exception.

Technology has long been a savior for Deaf people. Over and over, it has significantly improved their lives by helping them to obtain full access in a hearing world. For example, Deaf people were formerly denied certain jobs solely on the grounds that they could not use a telephone. Then telecommunication devices, which began with bulky teletype machines in the 1970s, were streamlined over the years to make it possible for Deaf people to use the telephone not only at home, but at school, at work, and on the road. Now—with the advent of computer modems, facsimile machines, relay systems, vibrating pagers, and other sophisticated devices—Deaf people can successfully communicate electronically with others as circumstances demand. With the addition of teleconferencing and streaming video, Deaf people can engage in more elaborate forms of visual communication as well.

Because of this evolving technology, an era of opportunity has emerged for Deaf people. Many of them have discovered that their interests and talents make them ideally suited to careers in the computer field. In the past, regardless of Federal laws mandating equality in the workplace, management often left Deaf workers in entry-level positions. They rationalized their refusal to give these workers an opportunity for upward mobility on the basis of communication difficulties. Now, the Internet, e-mail, and myriad computer applications—all remarkable tools for creativity and communication—have potentially leveled the playing field for Deaf people.

These rapid advances and changes, both in technology and in attitudes in the workplace, have necessitated the creation of a new sign language vocabulary for computer terms, many of which were themselves not familiar to any but the most technologically sophisticated insiders some ten or even five years ago. Certainly, this terminology had not become as commonplace in academic and career environments as it is now. Needing a rich new vocabulary for communication among themselves in this emerging technical field, Deaf people throughout the country have rapidly been creating new signs in American Sign Language and cleverly adapting existing ones, often on a rather ad hoc basis. It is only natural that when they travel and meet each other at conferences, they compare the signs they are currently using.

Unfortunately, they often find little consistency in the signs that have come into use in disparate locations. *Random House Webster's American Sign Language Computer Dictionary* strives to provide that consistency. It offers a rational, useful vocabulary for all those who are looking for conceptually correct signs for computer terms—signs that will enable all parts of the Deaf community to communicate as effectively in this new field as they now can in general.

This dictionary contains a wide-ranging collection of more than 1,200 computer terms of interest to Deaf computer users and their instructors. The terms, carefully selected, are for the most part those most likely to confront the beginning user, and the definitions have been written in a manner that a layperson can understand. But the entries also provide an up-to-date reference for those with more advanced computer skills.

Since Deaf people are both the users and developers of sign language, Deaf informants were interviewed in order to amass a collection of the signs they are actually using, particularly in the Washington, D.C., area. In addition, great care was given to make sure that the signs chosen for this book accurately represent the conceptual meanings of computer terms as used in the industry itself. Although some of the signs may have somewhat different meanings when used in other contexts, in this book, they are defined solely according to their technical use. The word *balance,* for example, given with its sign, is defined in the large Random House ASL dictionary as "equal distribution of weight, amount, etc.," while in this dictionary, it is defined specifically as "the visual arrangement of text and graphics to create a sense of equilibrium."

Computer technology is an incredibly fast-moving field. New terms are constantly being introduced and existing terms refined and enlarged upon. *Random House Webster's American Sign Language Computer Dictionary* provides a much-needed, up-to-date standard, making it possible for Deaf people to communicate efficiently about computers in their own language. Use of the signs in this book can increase the confidence of signers, who want to be sure that they have reduced the possibility of misunderstandings when communicating in diverse settings. It is hoped that this dictionary can provide solid guidance throughout the United States for interpreters, instructors, fellow students, employers, employees, friends and family, and Deaf people themselves.

Guide

How to Use This Dictionary

How to Find a Sign

Alphabetization

All the entries in this book, whether complete entries, entries for alternate signs, or cross-reference entries, are shown in **large boldface type** in a single alphabetical listing—e.g., **buffer, bug, built-in font, bullet, bulletin board**[1], **bulletin board**[2].

Complete Entries

Each complete entry has at least one *definition*, a description of *how to make the sign,* and one *illustration.* However, many of the entries are more complex than that. It is not unusual for a computer term to be constructed of several signs put together, just as a term in English can be composed of more than one word. The entry for **artificial intelligence,** for example, is made up of the two signs: **fake | smart,** and the word **broadband** of the three sequential signs: **share | communication | connect.** These component words are shown in **small boldface type** and each has an appropriate illustration and description of its sign.

Multiple Entries for the Same Word

When several entries are spelled the same way, each is marked with a small identifying superscript number. See, for example, the two entries for **character.** Note that the second of these is labeled "alternate sign." That is because it shares the meaning of the first, **character**[1], which contains the definition. Although the second therefore lacks a definition of its own, it has descriptions and illustrations for *alternate signs* that can be used instead of those shown at the earlier entry.

When identically spelled entries do have different meanings, each is defined, as at the four entries for **format,** the first three of which refer to preparing a disk to receive data and the fourth of which refers to the layout and general appearance of a document.

Any group of these entries may include one that is simply a cross reference to one or more other signs elsewhere in the alphabet—e.g., **hardware**[2], which says, "See signs for DEVICE[1,2]."

Cross References

Many entries include a list of other terms, shown in **smaller boldface,** for which the same sign (or compound sign) is applicable. Because the signs of ASL tend to represent broad concepts rather than specific English words, these additional terms are not always precise synonyms of the main entry. Often, their English equivalents do not even share a part of speech. However, they share the entry's concept in some way, and their meanings can all be conveyed with the same sign. The sign at **options,** for example, is also used to express **select.**

Where appropriate, these additional words are given usage labels (e.g., *informal, slang*) to indicate that in the context of certain social situations, the sign should be used with some caution.

A cross-reference entry at its own alphabetical listing does not show either a description or a sign. It may, however, give a definition when its meaning is not quite the same as that given for the main entry. A referential entry of this sort sends the reader to one or more complete entries by using small capital letters to point to the referent, where signs and descriptions will be found. Typical examples are the entry for **alphameric,** which says only "See sign for ALPHANUMERIC," and the entry for **abort,** which first defines and explains the word at length and then directs the reader to the appropriate main entry with the instruction, "See sign for CLOSE."

How to Make a Sign

Illustrations

Every complete entry and every entry labeled "alternate sign" contains at least one illustration. All the line drawings demonstrate how a right-handed signer would execute each sign as seen by the listener. The model's right hand is on the reader's left. A left-handed signer should transpose the hands, treating the picture as if it were a mirror image.

Descriptions

Each illustration is accompanied by a description. Within the description, italicized terms such as *A hand* and *C hand* refer to handshapes shown in the chart of the Manual Alphabet (p. xii). Terms such as *one hand* or *10 hand* refer to handshapes for numbers (p. xiii). Other special handshapes, such as *bent hand, open hand,* and *flattened C hand,* are also shown on page xiii.

An initialized sign (see, e.g., the entry for **centigrade**) is formed with one of the handshapes from the American Manual Alphabet (p. xii), and fingerspelled signs use the Manual Alphabet to spell out shortened forms, such as initialisms and acronyms, as at **CD-ROM,** where the instruction reads, "Fingerspell: C-D-R-O-M."

Using the above conventions, descriptions give detailed instructions on how to make the sign. Typically included in the description are a sign's four standard component parts: (1) handshape, (2) location in relation to the body, (3) movement of the hands, and (4) orientation of the palms. A component can appear more than once. The instructions at **character set,** for example, in the description for the sign for **group,** are as follows, with the components numbered to correspond with the descriptions just given:

(1) Beginning with both C hands

(2) in front of the chest,

(4) palms facing each other,

(3) bring the hands away from each other in outward arcs

(4) while turning the palms in, ending with the little fingers near each other.

Note that because the orientation of the palms changes during the course of making this sign, it is accounted for more than once.

American Manual Alphabet

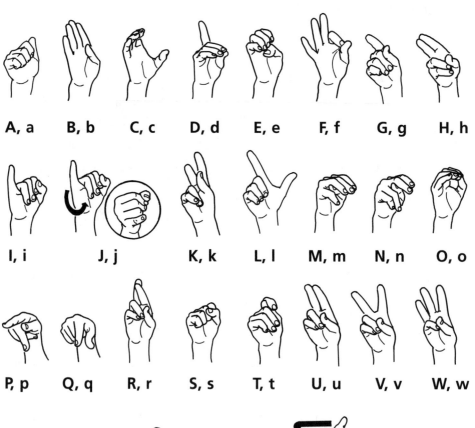

A, a	B, b	C, c	D, d	E, e	F, f	G, g	H, h

I, i	J, j	K, k	L, l	M, m	N, n	O, o

P, p	Q, q	R, r	S, s	T, t	U, u	V, v	W, w

X, x	Y, y	Z, z

Handshapes

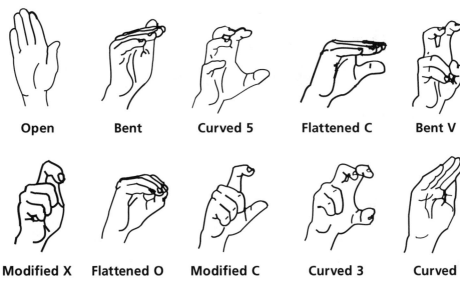

Open	Bent	Curved 5	Flattened C	Bent V
Modified X	Flattened O	Modified C	Curved 3	Curved

Numbers

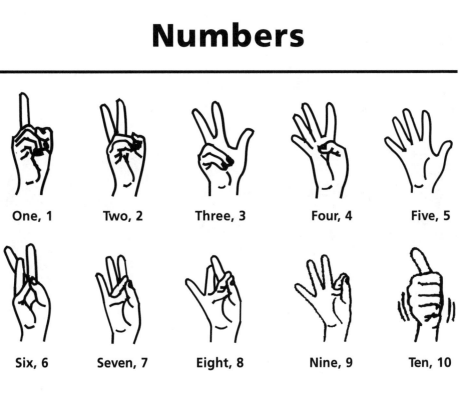

One, 1	Two, 2	Three, 3	Four, 4	Five, 5
Six, 6	Seven, 7	Eight, 8	Nine, 9	Ten, 10

abend Acronym for *Abnormal Ending*. The termination of a program caused by a system fault.

- **abend** Move the palm side of the right *A hand*, palm down, from the base to off the fingertips of the left *B hand*, palm in and fingers pointing right. Then move the right *open hand*, palm left and fingers pointing forward, straight down near the left fingertips.

Abnormal Ending See sign for ABEND.

abort To terminate a program or process prior to completion usually due to a hardware or software problem as compared with voluntarily *exiting* a program upon completion. Some programs allow the user to abort a process deliberately. See sign for CLOSE.

absolute address, machine address, or **real address** A fixed location in the main memory of a computer. Compare ADDRESS, BASE ADDRESS, RELATIVE ADDRESS.

- **specific** Beginning with the right *modified X hand* over the left *modified X hand*, move the right hand in a small circle and then down to touch the fingertips together in front of the chest.

- **address** Move both *A hands,* palms facing in, upward on each side of the chest with a double movement.

abstract or **summary** 1. To condense by discarding unnecessary detail. 2. A condensed version of a document or compilation. See sign for ACRONYM.

Accelerated Graphics Port See sign for AGP.

accelerator board An expansion board that can be added to a computer to increase its speed.

- **fast** Beginning with the extended index fingers of both *one hands* pointing forward in front of the chest, pull the hands back toward the chest while changing to *S hands*.

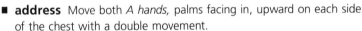

--- [sign continues] -->

accelerator board

- **board** Bring the little-finger side of the right *B hand*, palm left, sharply against the palm of the left *C hand* held in front of the chest, palm up.

access To call up or activate for use. Same sign used for **enter**.

- **enter** Move the back of the right *open hand* forward in a downward arc under the palm of the left *open hand*, both palms down.

access code See signs for PASSWORD[1,2].

access time or **seek time** The time lapse between a request for data from computer storage and the moment when it is available to the user.

- **enter** Move the back of the right *open hand* forward in a downward arc under the palm of the left *open hand*, both palms down.

- **time** Tap the bent index finger of the right *X hand*, palm down, with a double movement on the wrist of the downturned left hand.

accounting check A routine to assure that data has been entered and processed accurately.

- **count** Move the fingertips of the right *F hand*, palm down, across the upturned palm of the left *open hand* from the heel to the fingers with a repeated movement.

- **check** Move the extended right index finger sharply upward off the upturned palm of the left *open hand*.

accuracy The degree of exactness of computed results. Same sign used for **precision**.

- **exact** Beginning with the right *modified X hand* over the left *modified X hand*, move the right hand in a small circle and then down to touch fingertips together in front of the chest.

acronym A word formed from the first letter or letters of each word in a phrase or name. Same sign used for **abstract, shortcut,** or **summary**.

- **compress** Beginning with both *5 hands* in front of the chest, right hand above the left hand and fingers pointing in opposite directions, bring the hands toward each other while squeezing the fingers together, ending with the little-finger side of the right *S hand* on top of the thumb side of the left *S hand*.
- Fingerspell: A-C-R-O-N-Y-M

action 1. The performance of a particular operation. 2. The resulting activity from a given condition. Same sign used for **performance**. See sign for OPERATION.

activate, initiate, launch, or **start** To start some activity. Same sign used for **source**.

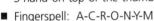

- **start** Beginning with the extended right index finger, palm down, inserted between the index and middle fingers of the left *open hand*, palm right and fingers pointing forward, twist the right hand, ending with palm angled forward.

active Referring to objects currently being displayed or used.

- **now** Bring both *Y hands*, palms facing up, downward in front of each side of the body.

- **ready** Move both *R hands* from in front of the right side of the body, palms down and fingers pointing forward, in a smooth movement to in front of the left side of the body.

active file A computer file currently being used.

- **now** Bring both *Y hands,* palms facing up, downward in front of each side of the body.

- **ready** Move both *R hands* from in front of the right side of the body, palms down and fingers pointing forward, in a smooth movement to in front of the left side of the body.

- **file** Slide the little-finger side of the right *B hand,* palm angled up, between the fingers of the left *5 hand,* palm facing in, first between the index and middle fingers and then between the middle and ring fingers.

---

active program Any of the computer programs currently being used.

- **now** Bring both *Y hands,* palms facing up, downward in front of each side of the body.

- **ready** Move both *R hands* from in front of the right side of the body, palms down and fingers pointing forward, in a smooth movement to in front of the left side of the body.

- **program** Move the middle finger of the right *P hand,* palm left, from the fingertips to the base of the left *open hand,* palm right and fingers pointing up. Repeat the movement on the back side of the left hand.

active window In a system that allows viewing multiple documents or programs on the screen, the document or window currently selected and available to the user.

- **now** Bring both *Y hands,* palms facing up, downward in front of each side of the body.

- **ready** Move both *R hands* from in front of the right side of the body, palms down and fingers pointing forward, in a smooth movement to in front of the left side of the body.

- **window** Beginning with the little-finger side of the right *B hand* on the index-finger side of the left *B hand,* both palms facing in and fingers pointing in opposite directions, move the right hand up and the left hand down simultaneously.

Ada A structured programming language developed for defense-related programming but not used anymore.

- Fingerspell: A-D-A

adapter Any hardware device or software routine that makes disparate hardware or software elements compatible.

- **change**[1] With the palm sides of both *modified X hands* facing each other, twist the wrists in opposite directions in order to reverse positions.

- **person marker** Move both *open hands*, palms facing each other, downward along the sides of the body.

adapter card

---

adapter card[1] An expansion board that is required to support a particular device.

- **change**[1] With the palm side of both *modified X hands* facing each other, twist the wrists in opposite directions in order to reverse positions.

- **card** Beginning with the fingertips of both *L hands* touching in front of the chest, palms facing forward, bring the hands apart to in front of each shoulder, and then pinch each thumb and index finger together.

---

adapter card[2] (alternate sign)

- **match** Beginning with both *5 hands* in front of each side of the chest, palms facing in, bring the hands together, ending with the bent fingers of both hands meshed together in front of the chest.

- **card** Beginning with the fingertips of both *L hands* touching in front of the chest, palms facing forward, bring the hands apart to in front of each shoulder, and then pinch each thumb and index finger together.

---

add-on A hardware or software supplement that serves to enhance performance of an existing program or device.

- **add-to** Swing the right *5 hand* upward from the right side of the body while changing into a *flattened O hand,* ending with the right index finger touching the little-finger side of the left *flattened O hand* in front of the chest, both palms facing in.

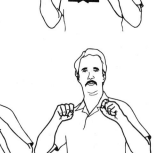

---- [sign continues] ---➤

■ **on** Bring the palm of the right *open hand* downward on the back of the left *open hand* held in front of the body, both palms facing down.

address A specific location in a computer system, identified by a name, number, or code label. Compare ABSOLUTE ADDRESS, BASE ADDRESS, RELATIVE ADDRESS.

■ **address** Move both *A hands,* palms facing in, upward on each side of the chest with a double movement.

address bus A set of wires that convey address data, running from the central processing unit (CPU) to random-access memory (RAM).

■ **address** Move both *A hands,* palms facing in, upward on each side of the chest with a double movement.

■ **bus** Beginning with the little-finger side of the right *B hand* touching the index-finger side of the left *B hand,* palms facing in opposite directions, move the right hand back toward the right shoulder.

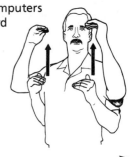

advanced power management A feature in most computers that powers down the screen and, in some cases, the hard drive when input has been suspended for a set interval, such as ten minutes.

■ **advance** Move both *bent hands,* palms facing each other, from near each side of the head upward a short distance in deliberate arcs.

---- [sign continues] ---➤

- **electric** Tap the knuckles of the index fingers of both *X hands* together, palms facing in, with a double movement.

- **control** Beginning with both *modified X hands* in front of each side of the body, right hand forward of the left hand and palms facing each other, move the hands forward and back with a repeated movement.

AGP Initialism for *Accelerated Graphics Port*. A graphics standard for displaying 3-D images.
- Fingerspell: A-G-P

---

alarm A warning system that is activated whenever a critical deviation from normal conditions occurs.
- **alarm** Tap the extended index finger of the right hand, palm forward, against the left *open hand*, palm right, with a repeated movement.

ALGOL Acronym for *Algorithmic Language*. One of the first programming languages to encourage structured programming.
- Fingerspell: A-L-G-O-L

---

algorithm A set of precise instructions for performing a specific task that must have a finite number of steps and a definite stopping place.
- **algorithm** Move the right *A hand* downward on the palm of the left *open hand,* palm right, while changing into an *M hand,* palm down.

Algorithmic Language See sign for ALGOL.

---

alias An alternative name that is easily remembered and related to its purpose, assigned to a file or block of data used in a spreadsheet.
- **search** Move the right *C hand*, palm left, with a double circular movement in front of the face.

---- [sign continues] ------------------>

■ **name** Tap the middle-finger side of the right *H* hand across the index-finger side of the left *H* hand with a double movement.

align The placement of type in a line, as flush right, centered, justified, etc.

■ **align** Move the little-finger side of the right *B* hand, palm left and fingers pointing forward, forward with a wavy movement along the extended left index finger, palm right and finger pointing forward.

allocate[1] To assign computer resources for performing a specific job. Same sign used for **partition, segment**. Related form: **allocation**.

■ **parts** Slide the little-finger side of the right *open hand*, palm left, with a double movement across the palm of the left *open hand*, palm up, moving to a different section of the left hand each time.

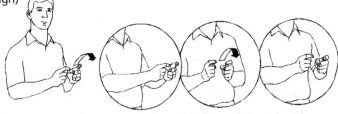

allocate[2] (alternate sign) Related form: **allocation**.

■ **donate** Move both *X hands* from in front of the left side of the body, palms facing each other, forward in simultaneous arcs. Repeat in front of the right side of the body.

alphabetic Referring to data that consists of letters and special symbols.

■ **alphabet** With the right hand, palm forward, sequentially form the first three manual alphabet letters in front of the right shoulder, moving the hand slightly to the right after each letter. Then move the right *5 hand*, palm down, to the right in front of the right shoulder while wiggling the fingers.

alphabetical

---

alphabetical/numeric See sign for ALPHANUMERIC.

---

alphameric See sign for ALPHANUMERIC.

---

alphanumeric or **alphameric** Short for *alphabetical/numeric*; descriptive of data that may contain both letters and numbers.

- Fingerspell: A-B-C

- **spell** Move the right *5 hand*, palm down, to the right in front of the right shoulder while wiggling the fingers.

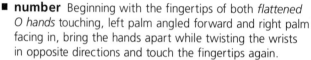

- **and** Move the right *5 hand*, palm in and fingers pointing left, from in front of the left side of the body to the right while closing the fingers to a *flattened O hand*.

- **number** Beginning with the fingertips of both *flattened O hands* touching, left palm angled forward and right palm facing in, bring the hands apart while twisting the wrists in opposite directions and touch the fingertips again.

---

alternate current In data communications, the process of switching the path to another location when the normal path is not available.

- **other** Beginning with the right *10 hand* in front of the chest, palm down, flip the hand over to the right, ending with palm up.

- **electric** Tap the knuckles of the index fingers of both *X hands* together, palms facing in, with a double movement.

- **path** Move both *open hands* from in front of each side of the body, palms facing each other, forward with a parallel movement.

Alt key A keyboard key that is used in conjunction with other keys to modify their actions or to execute commands.

- Fingerspell: A-L-T
- **key** Push the extended thumb of the right *10 hand* downward a short distance in front of the right side of the body.

ALU Acronym for *arithmetic-logic unit.* The part of the central processing unit (CPU) that performs arithmetic computations and comparison operations.

- Fingerspell: A-L-U

American Standard Code for Information Interchange See sign for ASCII.

analog 1. Descriptive of data represented as a continuous variable, such as sound or an electrical impulse, as contrasted with digital, which has values measured at distinct intervals. 2. Denoting a device that measures changing conditions and converts them into quantities: *an analog computer; an analog monitor.*

- **analog** Move both *A hands* from in front of the right side of the body, palms facing down, across to the left side of the body in arcs and then back to the right again.

analog-to-digital converter A device that converts analog signals, such as those from a telephone, to digital data that can be processed by the computer.

- **analog-to-digital** Touch the heel of the right *A hand*, palm forward, to the thumb of the left *5 hand*, palm in. Then, touch the heel of the right *D hand*, palm forward, to the index finger of the left *5 hand*, palm in.

- **convert**[1] With both *C hands* in front of the chest, thumbs touching, turn the right hand.

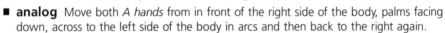

- **person marker** Move both *open hands*, palms facing each other, downward along the sides of the body.

analysis The investigation of a program by some consistent, systematic procedure to explore the nature of its actions or to resolve a problem.

- **analyze** With both *bent V hands* near each other in front of the chest, palms facing down, move the fingers apart from each other with a repeated movement.

anchor **1.** The starting point for a block of copy for editing, printing, etc. **2.** A position for placement of extraneous matter in a document, such as graphics or sound.

- **anchor** Beginning with the thumb side of the right *X hand,* palm facing down, against the palm of the left *3 hand,* palm facing right and fingers pointing forward, bring the right hand downward in an arc, ending with the palm facing left.

AND A connector in computer programming that is used to return a value of *true* if both of the statements it joins are true; used in a Boolean search.

- **and** Move the right *5 hand,* palm in and fingers pointing left, from in front of the left side of the body to the right while closing the fingers to a *flattened O hand.*

annotation A comment, note, or descriptive remark added to a program or flowchart.

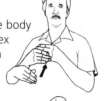

- **add-to** Swing the right *5 hand* upward from the right side of the body while changing into a *flattened O hand,* ending with the right index finger touching the little-finger side of the left *flattened O hand* in front of the chest, both palms facing in.

- **comment** Move the extended right index finger from in front of the mouth, palm in and finger pointing left, forward in a small arc.

anti-virus program A program designed to detect unauthorized and unwanted instructions, as from downloaded software or Internet sources, that might disrupt a computer's normal operation.

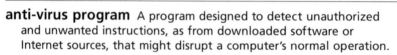

- **prevent** With the little-finger side of the right *B hand* against the index-finger side of the left *B hand,* palms facing in opposite directions, move the hands forward a short distance.

- Fingerspell: V-I-R-U-S

---- [sign continues] -->

■ **program** Move the middle finger of the right
P hand, palm left, from the fingertips to the base
of the left *open hand*, palm right and fingers pointing
up. Repeat the movement on the back side of the
left hand.

APL Acronym for *A Programming Language*. An interactive computer programming language notably proficient for its problem-solving applications. In its simplest mode of operation, APL performs the functions of an intelligent calculator.

■ Fingerspell: A-P-L

---

append See sign for ATTACH.

---

application or **program** An electronic list of instructions that a computer can respond to so as to perform a particular task. Same sign used for **programming**.

■ **program** Move the middle finger of the right
P hand, palm left, from the fingertips to the base
of the left *open hand*, palm right and fingers
pointing up. Repeat the movement on the back
side of the left hand.

---

application program or **application software**
1. A computer program designed for a particular use by an end user, such as a word processing or spreadsheet program. 2. The particular task to which an application program is applied, such as accounting, word processing, or desktop publishing.

■ **apply** Move the fingers of the right *V hand,* palm forward, downward on each side of the extended left index finger, pointing up in front of the chest.

■ **program** Move the middle finger of the right *P hand*, palm left, from the fingertips to the base of the left *open hand*, palm right and fingers pointing up. Repeat the movement on the back side of the left hand.

---

application software See sign for APPLICATION PROGRAM.

---

approximation A value which is only nearly correct; a number that has been rounded or truncated.

■ **number** Beginning with the fingertips of both *flattened O hands* touching, palms facing in opposite directions, bring the hands apart slightly while twisting the wrists in opposite directions and touch the fingertips again.

---- [sign continues] ---->

- **approximate** Move the right *5 hand*, palm forward, in a circle in front of the right shoulder with a double movement.

A Programming Language See sign for APL.

architecture **1.** The physical structure of a computer. See also CLOSED ARCHITECTURE, OPEN ARCHITECTURE. **2.** The overall design of a software program.

- **architecture** Beginning with the thumbs of both *A hands* touching in front of the face, palms forward, move the hands apart and down a short distance at an angle, and then straight down to in front of each side of the chest.

archival backup or **incremental backup** A type of backup in which only files that have been modified since the last backup are copied.

- **save** Tap the fingers of the right *V hand* with a double movement on the back of the left *S hand*, both palms facing in.

- **backup** Beginning with the right *10 hand*, palm down, beside the left *10 hand*, palm right, move the right hand clockwise in an arc and then forward to the heel of the left hand, ending with the right palm facing left.

archive **1.** To save files for long-term storage. **2.** A disk, tape, or directory that contains files that have been backed up.

- **save** Tap the fingers of the right *V hand* with a double movement on the back of the left *S hand*, both palms facing in.

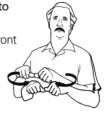

area search The examination of a large group of documents to select those that pertain to one group.

- **area** Beginning with the thumbs of both *A hands* touching in front of the chest, palms facing down, move the hands apart in a backward circular movement until they touch again near the chest.

---- [sign continues] -->

■ **search** Move the right *C hand*, palm left, with a double circular movement in front of the face.

arithmetic, calculate, or **compute** Mathematics; the addition, subtraction, multiplication, and division of numbers.

■ **multiply** Brush the back of the right *V hand* across the palm side of the left *V hand,* both palms facing up, as the hands cross with a double movement in front of the chest.

arithmetic-logic unit See sign for ALU.

arrangement The way items are located or displayed in a set or array.

■ **arrange** Move both *open hands* from in front of the left side of the body, palms facing each other and fingers pointing forward, in a series of small arcs to in front of the right side of the body.

array An ordered arrangement of objects all of which are the same size and type.

■ **array** Bring both *A hands,* palms facing down, up and down simultaneously in front of each side of the chest with a double movement.

artificial intelligence[1] The ability of a computer to simulate human intelligence.

■ Fingerspell: A-I

artificial intelligence[2] (alternate sign)

■ **fake** Beginning with the index finger of the right *4 hand* touching the right side of the forehead, move the hand forward in several short movements.

■ **smart** Bring the bent middle finger of the right *5 hand* from touching the forehead, palm in, forward while turning the palm forward.

15

ASCII Acronym for *American Standard Code for Information Interchange*. A standardized code for representing English characters as numbers making it possible to transfer data from one computer to another. Compare EBCDIC.

■ Fingerspell: A-S-C-I-I

assemble[1] or **assembly** To convert computer program instructions from programming language (**assembly language**) into machine language that can be understood by the computer.

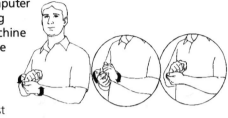

■ **assemble[1]** With the palm side of the right *T hand* on top of the palm side of the left *A hand* in front of the body, twist the wrists in opposite directions to reverse positions.

assemble[2] or **assembly** (alternate sign)

■ **assemble[2]** Beginning with the thumbs of both *A hands* together in front of the chest, both palms facing down, bring the hands apart to each side with a double movement.

assembler A program that translates programming language into simple instructions that are understood directly by a computer.

■ **assemble[2]** Beginning with the thumbs of both *A hands* together in front of the chest, both palms facing down, bring the hands apart to each side with a double movement.

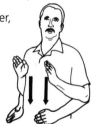

■ **person marker** Move both *open hands*, palms facing each other, downward along the sides of the body.

assembly See signs for ASSEMBLE[1,2].

assembly language See sign for ASSEMBLE[1].

assign To give value to a variable.

■ **give** Move the right *X hand* from in front of the right side of the chest, palm left, forward in a large arc.

asterisk A character used to add a note or to show an omission in a search string, especially of two or more characters. See sign for WILDCARD[1].

asynchronous Referring to data communication that provides a variable time interval between characters during transmission. Compare SYNCHRONOUS.

- **not** Bring the extended thumb of the right *10 hand* from under the chin, palm left, forward with a deliberate movement.

- **standard** Beginning with both *Y hands* in front of the left side of the body, palms facing down, move the hands smoothly across to in front of the right side of the body.

attach or **append** 1. To add something to the end, such as one file to another or a field to the end of a record. 2. Refers to how files are sent through e-mail. Related form: **attachment**.

- **add-to** Swing the right *5 hand* upward from the right side of the body while changing into a *flattened O hand,* ending with the right index finger touching the little-finger side of the left *flattened O hand* in front of the chest, both palms facing in.

autoexec.bat Shortened form of *automatic execute batch file.* The name of the file that is automatically executed by DOS when a computer running DOS is turned on.

- **itself** Bring the knuckles of the right *10 hand*, palm left, firmly against the side of the extended left index finger, palm right and finger pointing up in front of the chest.

- **run** Brush the palm of the right *open hand* upward with a double movement across the left *open hand*, palms facing each other and fingers pointing forward.

- **period** With the right index finger and thumb pinched together, palm forward, push the right hand forward a short distance.

- Fingerspell: B-A-T

automation

automation[1] **1.** Processes accomplished by mechanical or electronic devices. **2.** The replacement of human workers by machines.

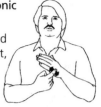

- **automatic**[1] Move the extended right curved index finger back and forth on the back of the left *open hand* with a repeated movement, both palms facing in.

automation[2] (alternate sign)

- **automatic**[2] Move the extended right curved index finger, palm in, back and forth on the side of extended left index finger, palm down.

AutoPlay The ability of a computer to detect the presence of a CD and run it without user commands.

- **itself** Bring the knuckles of the right *10 hand*, palm left, firmly against the side of the extended left index finger, palm right and finger pointing up in front of the chest.

- **run** Brush the palm of the right *open hand* upward with a double movement across the left *open hand,* palms facing each other and fingers pointing forward.

autosave Refers to a feature in which the computer program automatically saves data files at predetermined intervals.

- **itself** Bring the knuckles of the right *10 hand,* palm left, firmly against the side of the extended left index finger, palm right and finger pointing up in front of the chest.

- **save** Tap the fingers of the right *V hand* with a double movement on the back of the left *S hand*, both palms facing in.

auxiliary storage See signs for MASS STORAGE[1,2].

available Refers to the amount of space remaining on a disk that can be used to store data.

■ **bare** Move the bent middle finger of the right *5 hand*, palm down, in a double circle on the back of the left *open hand*, palm down.

back A command telling the computer to go back one page on a Web site. See sign for BACKSPACE.

background In multitasking computers, the part of the screen that cannot accept interactive input from the user. Compare FOREGROUND.

- **background** In quick succession tap the index-finger side of the right *B hand* and then *G hand,* palm facing forward, against the left *open hand,* palm facing right.

backslash **1.** A character (\) used to separate directory and file names in some operating systems. **2.** A keyboard key that inserts this character.

- **slash** Bring the right *B hand,* palm left, from in front of the right shoulder downward to the left with a deliberate movement.

- **back** Beginning with the right *10 hand* in front of the chest, palm down, twist the hands upward to the right, ending with the palm up and the extended thumb pointing right.

backspace or **backward** **1.** A keyboard operation that moves the cursor one place to the left, allowing modification of what has already been typed. **2. Backspace** A keyboard key that moves the cursor one place to the left when pressed. In many programs, this is a destructive key that deletes the character to the left as it is pressed. Same sign used for **back.**

- **back** Beginning with the right *10 hand* in front of the chest, palm down, twist the hand upward to the right, ending with the palm up and the extended thumb pointing right.

backup **1.** A duplicate copy of computer data or a software program for use if the original fails. **2.** Designating such a copy. **3. back up** To make such a copy. Compare RESTORE.

- **backup** Beginning with the right *10 hand,* palm down, beside the left *10 hand,* palm right, move the right hand clockwise in an arc and then forward to the heel of the left hand, ending with the right palm facing left.

backup copy A copy of a file or data that is kept for reference in case the original is destroyed.

- **backup** Beginning with the right *10 hand,* palm down, beside the left *10 hand,* palm right, move the right hand clockwise in an arc and then forward to the heel of the left hand, ending with the right palm facing left.

- **file** Slide the little-finger side of the right *B hand,* palm angled up, between the fingers of the left *5 hand,* palm facing in, first between the index and middle fingers and then between the middle and ring fingers.

backward See sign for BACKSPACE.

bad sector A portion of a disk that cannot be used because it is flawed.

- **bad** Move the fingers of the right *open hand* from the mouth, palm in, downward while flipping the palm quickly down as the hand moves.

- **parts** Slide the little-finger side of the right *open hand,* palm left, with a double movement across the palm of the left *open hand,* palm up, moving to a different section of the left hand each time.

balance The visual arrangement of text and graphics to create a sense of equilibrium.

- **balance** With a simultaneous double movement bring the right *open hand* and the left *open hand,* both palms facing down, up and down in front of each side of the chest, shifting the entire torso slightly with each movement.

bandwidth The amount of data that can be transmitted in a fixed amount of time.

- Fingerspell: B-A-N-D
- **wide** Beginning with both *open hands* in front of each side of the body, palms facing each other and fingers pointing forward, move the hands apart to the sides of the body, ending with palms angled forward.

bar[1] or **toolbar** A feature on the display screen, usually along the top, bottom, or side but sometimes floating, containing icons or buttons that represent commonly used commands that activate functions when clicked upon.

- **bar** Move the fingers of the right *G hand*, palm forward, from left to right in front of the chest.

---

bar[2] or **toolbar** (alternate sign)

- Fingerspell: T-O-O-L
- **bar** Move the fingers of the right *G hand*, palm forward, from left to right in front of the chest.

---

bar code or **universal product code** A pattern of thick and thin lines and spaces that represent characters that can be read by a scanner. The bar code identifies the item to which it is affixed.

- **stripes** Pull the right *4 hand*, palm in and fingers pointing left, from left to right in front of the chest with a double movement.

---

bar code reader A scanner, whether handheld or stationery, that transfers the signal from a bar code to a computer, which matches the code to a price, inventory unit, address, etc.

- **stripes** Pull the right *4 hand*, palm in and fingers pointing left, from left to right in front of the chest with a double movement.

- **read** Bring the fingers of the right *V hand* downward with a double movement across the palm of the left *open hand* held in front of the chest, palm facing up and fingers pointing forward.

---

base or **base number** The number of digits used in a counting system.

- **base** Move the right *B hand*, palm facing left, in a flat circle under the left *open hand*, palm facing down.

base address An address that serves as a reference point for other addresses. Compare ABSOLUTE ADDRESS; ADDRESS; RELATIVE ADDRESS.

- **base** Move the right *B hand,* palm facing left, in a flat circle under the left *open hand,* palm facing down.

- **address** Move both *A hands,* palms facing in, upward on each side of the chest with a double movement.

---

base eight See sign for OCTAL.

---

baseline The imaginary line on which a row of type rests and by which position is determined.

- **base** Move the right *B hand,* palm facing left, in a flat circle under the left *open hand,* palm facing down.

- **line** Beginning with the extended little fingers of both *I hands* touching in front of the chest, palms facing in, move both hands outward.

---

base number See sign for BASE.

---

base sixteen See sign for HEXADECIMAL.

---

base ten See sign for DECIMAL[1].

---

base two See sign for BINARY.

BASIC Acronym for *Beginner's All-purpose Symbolic Instruction Code.* A relatively simple programming language developed in the 1960s, designed to make programming easier, especially for novices.

- Fingerspell: B-A-S-I-C

Basic Input/Output System or BIOS Software that is built into a computer to control input devices, like the keyboard and the mouse, and output devices, like the display screen and the printer.

- Fingerspell: B-I-O-S

BAT The file extension identifying batch files.
- Fingerspell: B-A-T

---

batch file 1. A text file that contains lists of operating system commands that are processed as a unit. **2.** In DOS systems, files that end with a .BAT extension.

- **group** Beginning with both *C hands* in front of the chest, palms facing each other, bring the hands away from each other in outward arcs while turning the palms in, ending with the little fingers near each other.

- **file** Slide the little-finger side of the right *B hand*, palm angled up, between the fingers of the left *5 hand,* palm facing in, first between the index and middle fingers and then between the middle and ring fingers.

---

batch processing Processing a series of programs that have been accumulated over time all at one time.

- **group** Beginning with both *C hands* in front of the chest, palms facing each other, bring the hands away from each other in outward arcs while turning the palms in, ending with the little fingers near each other.

- **process** Beginning with both *open hands* in front of the body, palms facing in, left fingers pointing right and right fingers pointing left, and the left hand closer to the chest than the right hand, move the left over the right hand and then the right over the left hand in an alternating movement.

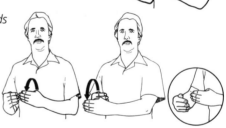

---

battery backup A computer's internal battery that keeps track of the current time and other configuration information even when the computer is unplugged.

- **battery** Tap the knuckles of both *bent V hands* together, palms facing in, with a double movement in front of the chest.

- **backup** Beginning with the right *10 hand,* palm down, beside the left *10 hand,* palm right, move the right hand clockwise in an arc and then forward to the heel of the left hand, ending with the right palm facing left.

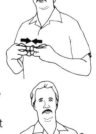

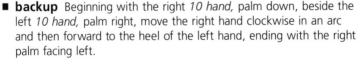

battery pack A battery, usually rechargeable, that is used to run a laptop computer or other portable device when it is not plugged into an electric outlet.

■ **bring** Move both *open hands*, palms up, from in front of the right side of the body in large arcs to the left side of the body.

■ **battery** Tap the knuckles of both *bent V hands* together, palms facing in, with a double movement in front of the chest.

■ **box** Beginning with both *open hands* in front of each side of the chest, palms facing each other and fingers pointing forward, move the hands deliberately in opposite directions, ending with the left hand near the chest and the right hand several inches forward of the left hand, both palms facing in.

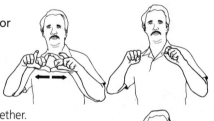

baud or **baud rate** The measure of transmission speed, equivalent to about 1 bit per second.

■ Fingerspell: B-A-U-D

baud rate See sign for BAUD.

bay A space in a computer cabinet where a hardware device such as a floppy disk, CD, or tape drive has been or can be installed.

■ **card** Beginning with the fingertips of both *L hands* touching in front of the chest, palms facing forward, bring the hands apart to in front of each shoulder, and then pinch each thumb and index finger together.

■ **insert** Slide the little-finger side of the right *open hand*, palm in and fingers angled to the left, between the middle finger and ring finger of the left *open hand* held in front of the chest, palm right and fingers pointing up.

■ **computer**[1] Move the thumb side of the right *C hand*, palm left, from touching the lower part of the extended left arm upward to touch the upper arm.

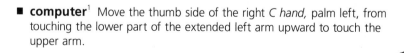

BBS

BBS See signs for BULLETIN BOARD[1,2].

Beginner's All-purpose Symbolic Instruction Code See sign for BASIC.

benchmark A standard by which computers, programs, peripherals, etc., can be compared in performance tests.

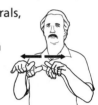

- **measure** Beginning with the thumbs of both *Y hands* touching in front of the chest, palms facing down in front of the chest, bring the hands apart.

beta test The use of a new computer program by a selected group of users in order to discover any problems that need to be corrected before releasing the program to the public.

- Fingerspell: B-E-T-A
- **test** With both extended index fingers pointing forward in front of the chest, palms down, bring the hands downward while bending the index fingers into *X hands* and continuing down while extending the index fingers again.

binary or **base two** A number system in base 2, using two digits. Binary computer systems use zeros and ones, which can be combined to express any number.

- **binary** Move the right *B hand*, palm forward, under the left *open hand*, palm down and fingers pointing right, changing into a *V hand* as it moves.

binary digit See sign for BIT.

binary file A file in machine code that only a computer can use and ending with the BIN file extension.

- Fingerspell: B-I-N

binder See signs for LINKER[1,2].

BIOS See sign for BASIC INPUT/OUTPUT SYSTEM.

bit Short for *binary digit*. The basic unit in the binary system.

- **bit** Beginning with the thumb side of the right *B hand*, palm angled forward, against the palm of the left *open hand*, palm right, move the right hand downward, touching first at the fingertips and then at the heel of the left hand.

bitmap See sign for BITMAPPED IMAGE.

bitmapped image or **bitmap** A graphic image composed of tiny dots called pixels.

- **dots** Touch the fingertips of the right *C hand* on the palm of the left *open hand* held in front of the chest, palm right and fingers pointing up, from the fingertips to the heel.

- **picture** Move the right *C hand*, palm forward, from near the right side of the face downward, ending with the index-finger side of the right *C hand* against the palm of the left *open hand* held in front of the chest, palm right.

blank The absence of data in a computer file or on a floppy disk.

- **empty** Move the bent middle fingertip of the right *5 hand* across the back of the left *open hand* from the wrist to off the fingertips, both palms facing down.

block, highlight, or **select** To isolate selected text for some action, as in a word processing document.

- **select** Beginning with the thumb side of the right *5 hand,* palm forward, near the left *open hand* palm right and fingers pointing up, pull the right hand back to touch the left palm while pinching the index finger and thumb together.

boilerplate Prewritten text that is used over and over in various documents such as form letters or legal documents. See sign for TEMPLATE.

bold or **boldface** Descriptive of type having thick, heavy lines.

- **thicker** Beginning with the right *G hand* in front of the right shoulder, palm forward, spread the thumb and index finger apart.

- **letter** Touch the extended thumb of the right *10 hand* to the lips, palm in, and then move the thumb downward to touch the thumb of the left *10 hand* held in front of the chest, palm in.

boldface See sign for BOLD.

bomb See signs for CRASH[1,2].

bookmark, favorite, or **place marker** A user-specified reference marker in a browser that allows instant selection of an Internet site from another location.

- **book** Beginning with the palms of both *open hands* together in front of the chest, fingers angled forward, bring the hands apart at the top while keeping the little fingers together.

- **insert** Slide the little-finger side of the right *open hand*, palm in and fingers angled to the left, between the middle finger and ring finger of the left *open hand* held in front of the chest, palm right and fingers pointing up.

Boolean A logic system utilizing operators such as AND, OR, and NOT and based on the return of one of two variables.

- Fingerspell: B-O-O-L-E-A-N

boot[1] To start a computer by turning on the power, causing it to load its operating system.

- **kick** Bring the right *B hand* upward to strike the index-finger side of the right hand against the little-finger side of the left *open hand* held in front of the chest, palm angled up and fingers pointing forward.

boot[2] (alternate sign)

- **kick** Bring the right *B hand* upward to strike the index-finger side of the right hand against the little-finger side of the left *open hand* held in front of the chest, palm angled up and fingers pointing forward.

- **start** Beginning with the extended right index finger, palm down, inserted between the index and middle fingers of the left *open hand*, palm right and fingers pointing forward, twist the right hand, ending with palm angled forward.

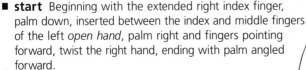

boot disk or **bootstrap** A disk, device, or routine that loads the operating system into a computer, enabling it to operate.

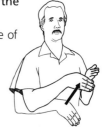

■ **kick** Bring the right *B hand* upward to strike the index-finger side of the right hand against the little-finger side of the left *open hand* held in front of the chest, palm angled up and fingers pointing forward.

■ **disk** Move the fingertips of the right *D hand,* palm facing down and index finger pointing forward, in a double circle on the upturned left *open hand.*

bootstrap See sign for BOOT DISK.

branch The selection of one or more possible paths in the flow of control based on some criterion. See sign for CHANNEL.

branch point A place in a program where a branch is selected.

■ **jump**[1] Beginning with both *bent V* hands in front of the left side of the chest, palms facing down, move the hands in a arc to in front of the right side of the body.

■ **point** Move the extended right index finger forward to touch the left extended index finger held up in front of the chest.

breakpoint In programming, a place in a program where the computer temporarily stops running.

■ **intermission** Slide the index-finger side of the right *B hand,* palm down, between the middle and ring fingers of the left *5 hand,* palm facing in and fingers pointing right.

---- [sign continues] --➤

breakpoint

- **point** Move the extended right index finger forward to touch the left extended index finger held up in front of the chest.

brightness 1. In computer graphics, the relative presence or absence of shading. 2. The display screen intensity, which can normally be varied by the user through hardware or software controls.

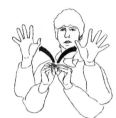

- **bright** Beginning with the fingertips of both *flattened O hands* touching in front of the chest, palms facing each other, move the hands quickly upward in arcs to above each shoulder while opening to *5 hands*.

broadband A type of high-speed data transmission in which the bandwidth is shared by simultaneous signals. Compare DIAL-UP ACCESS.

- **share** Move the little-finger side of the right *open hand*, palm in, back and forth with a double movement at the base of the index finger of the left *open hand*, palm in.

- **communication** Move both *C hands*, palms facing each other, forward and back from the mouth with an alternating movement.

- **connect** Beginning with both *curved 5 hands* in front of each side of the body, palms facing each other, bring the hands together while touching the thumb and index fingertips of each hand and intersecting with each other.

broadcast or **multicast** In data communications, the dissemination of information to a number of stations simultaneously.

- **multicast** With the palm side of the right *modified X hand* on the back of the left *open hand* held across the body, flick the right index finger forward. Move the right hand slightly and flick the right index finger forward in a different direction.

browse 1. To look for a specific files on the hard drive. 2. To look for something on the Internet. See sign for SEARCH.

browser See sign for Web browser.

bubble Any of the magnetized dots (bubbles) that rest on a thin film of semiconductor material, used for storing information. Bubble memory is no longer widely used.

- **bubble** Beginning with both *F hands* in front of the chest, palms facing forward, move the right hand above the left hand and the left hand above the right hand as the hands move upward in front of the chest with an alternating movement.

buffer An area for temporary storage of data being transferred from one device to another.

- **buffer** Beginning with the little-finger side of the right open hand, palm angled left, in the space at the base of the index finger and thumb of the left flattened C hand, palm facing up, rock the right hand from side to side with a double movement.

bug A defect in a computer system or program that keeps it from working properly.

- **insect** With the extended thumb of the right *3 hand* on the nose, palm left, bend the extended index and middle fingers with a double movement.

built-in font See sign for Resident font.

bullet a heavy dot or other symbol used at the beginning of each of a series of lines, paragraphs, or other items of information to set them off.

- **list**[1] Touch the little-finger side of the right *bent hand*, palm in, from the fingertips of the left *open hand* down the left forearm.

- **bullet** Touch the fingertips of the right index finger and thumb pinched together from the fingers to the heel of the left *open hand* held in front of the chest, palm right and fingers pointing up.

bulletin board[1], bulletin board system, BBS, post,
or **publish a message** A message center, often serving special interest groups, that is accessed by computer users via telephone data lines for the exchange of information.

- **bulletin board** Push the thumbs of both *10 hands,* forward with a short movement, palms facing forward, first in front of each shoulder and then in front of each side of the body.

bulletin board[2], bulletin board system, or BBS (alternate sign)

- Fingerspell: B-B-S

bulletin board system See signs for BULLETIN BOARD[1,2].

bump See sign for INCREMENT.

bundled software Software sold as a package together with a new computer.

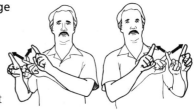

- **different-different** Beginning with both extended index fingers crossed in front of the right side of the chest, palms facing forward, bring the hands apart from each other with a deliberate movement. Repeat in front of the left side of the chest.

- **gather** Beginning with both *curved 5 hands* in front of each side of the chest, palms facing each other, bring the fingers together in front of the body.

- Fingerspell: S-W

burn To use electrical pulses to program disks, such as CD-ROMs, with programmable memory. Same sign used for **laser**.

- **laser** With the index finger of the right *L hand* pointing at the palm of the left *open hand*, move the right hand back and forth with a double movement.

bus A channel or path through electrical wires for transferring data and electrical signals to and from various parts of a computer system.

- **bus** Beginning with the little-finger side of the right *B hand* touching the index-finger side of the left *B hand,* palms facing in opposite directions, move the right hand back toward the right shoulder.

business software Programs specifically designed for business applications, including electronic spreadsheets, payroll programs, and accounting programs.

- **business** Brush the base of the right *B hand,* palm forward, with a repeated rocking movement on the back of the left *open hand,* palm down.

- Fingerspell: S-W

---

button 1. A key on the keyboard. 2. A graphical representation of a button that you activate by clicking on it with a mouse.

- **button** Push the extended thumb of the right *10 hand,* palm left, forward a short distance in front of the chest.

---

byte 1. A basic unit of data used by a computer consisting of eight bits. 2. The space required to store a single printer character.

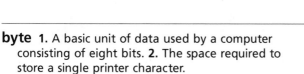

- **byte** Move the thumb side of the right *B hand,* palm forward and fingers pointing up, down the palm of the left *open hand,* palm right, touching first on the fingers and then on the heel.

C A programming language developed in the 1970s with the ability to manipulate a computer; similar to assembly language.

- Fingerspell: C

C++ An improved version of the C programming language that is easy to use and provides object-oriented features.

- Fingerspell: C
- **plus-plus** Place the side of the extended right index finger, palm facing down and finger pointing left, against the extended left index finger pointing up in front of the chest. Move the hands slightly to the right and repeat.

cable An electrical wire or bundle of wires used to connect two parts of a computer system together.

- **cable** Beginning with the index-finger side of both *C hands* touching in front of the body, palms down, bring the right hand outward to the right.

cache A temporary storage space for frequently accessed program instructions.

- Fingerspell: C-A-C-H-E

cache memory or **cache store** A specialized chip used with the computer's memory to provide a storage area that keeps frequently accessed data or program instructions readily available.

- Fingerspell: C-A-C-H-E
- **memory** Beginning with the fingertips of the right *curved hand* touching the right side of the forehead, palm down, bring the hand forward and down while closing the fingers into an *S hand*, palm in.

cache store See sign for CACHE MEMORY.

CAD Acronym for *computer-aided design*. A CAD system is a combination of hardware and software used by engineers and architects to design three-dimensional products. CAD software is used with a high-quality graphics monitor; a mouse, light pen, or digitizing tablet for drawing and a special printer or plotter for printing design specifications.

- Fingerspell: C-A-D

calculate See sign for ARITHMETIC.

calculator **1.** A handheld computer that performs mathematical calculations. **2.** A program on a computer that simulates a handheld calculator.

- **calculator** Alternately tap each fingertip of the right *5 hand* while moving up and down the upturned left *open hand* held in front of the body.

calendar A program that enables you to record events and appointments, often including electronic reminders of appointment times and of tasks to be competed.

- **calendar** Move the little-finger side of the right *C hand*, palm left, from the heel upward in an arc over the fingertips of the left *open hand*, palm in and fingers pointing up.

call or **invoke** To invoke a routine in a programming language.

- **call** Slap the fingers of the right *open hand* across the back of the left *S hand*, both palms down, dragging the right fingers upward and closing them into an *A hand* in front of the right shoulder.

camera-ready The final state of a publication before it is commercially printed; formerly referring to text and graphics on high-quality glossy paper that can easily be photographed but now usually referring to final, edited electronic files.

- **print** Bring the thumb side of the right *G hand*, palm down, against the left *open hand*, palm up, and pinch the right thumb and index finger together with a double movement.

- **ready** Move both *R hands* from in front of the left side of the body, palms facing each other and fingers pointing forward, in a smooth movement from right to left in front of the chest.

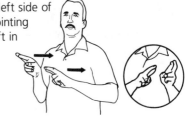

cancel A command to a computer to reverse a change made in an application or to stop a procedure.

- **cancel** With the extended right index finger, draw a large X across the upturned left *open hand*.

capacity The amount of storage available on a computer hard drive or disk.

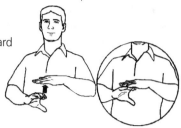

- **capacity** Bring the right *C hand*, palm left, upward under the left *open hand*, palm down and fingers pointing right.

---

caps Short for *capital letters*. See signs for UPPERCASE[1,2].

Caps Lock A keyboard key that causes all letters to become uppercase without having to press the Shift key each time. The number row and punctuation marks are not affected.

- **capital** Hold the right *modified C hand*, palm forward, in front of the right side of the body.

- **lock** Beginning with both *S hands* in front of the body, right hand above left and both palms facing down, turn the right hand over by twisting the wrist, ending with the back of the right *S hand*, palm up, on the back of the left *S hand*, palm down.

---

capture To save a particular state of a program, usually the information currently visible on a display screen. See sign for SAVE.

Carpal Tunnel Syndrome, repetitive motion injury, or **repetitive stress injury** A common form of repetitive strain injury produced by repeating the same small movements many times, such as typing for extended periods on a computer keyboard.

- **bone** With a double movement, tap the back of the right *bent V hand*, on the back of the left *S hand*, palm down.

- **wrist** With the bent middle finger and thumb of the right *5 hand* grasp each side of the left wrist.

- **hurt** Beginning with both extended index fingers pointing toward each other in front of the body, palms up, jab the fingers toward each other with a short double movement.

carrier Short for *carrier service provider*: A company offering telephone and data communications between points in a state or between countries.

- **bring** Move both *open hands*, palms up, from in front of the right side of the body in large arcs to the left side of the body.

- **person marker** Move both *open hands*, palms facing each other, downward along each side of the body.

cartridge A plug-in module inserted into a special slot in a computer.

- **card** Beginning with the fingertips of both *L hands* touching in front of the chest, palms forward, bring the hands apart to in front of each shoulder, and then pinch each thumb and index finger together.

- **cartridge** Push the fingers of the right *bent L hand* forward a short distance in front of the chest.

cascade See sign for OVERLAY.

case[1] A programming routine involving a complex set of decisions based on a single item.

- Fingerspell: C-A-S-E

case[2] (alternate sign)

- **case** Beginning with the right *G hand* in front of the chest, palm left, move the thumb and index finger apart with a double movement.

case sensitive Indicating a program's ability to distinguish between uppercase (capital) and lowercase (small) letters.

- Fingerspell: C-A-S-E

- **sensitive** Beginning with the bent middle finger of the right *5 hand* touching the right side of the chest, flick the wrist forward, ending with the palm facing down.

catalog, index, or **list** 1. An ordered compilation of items and sufficient information that make the items easily accessible. 2. To enter information into a table.

- **list**[1] Touch the little-finger side of the right *bent hand*, palm in, from the fingertips of the left *open hand* down the left forearm.

---

cathode ray tube See sign for DISPLAY SCREEN.

CD-E See signs for CD-ERASABLE[1,2].

CD-Erasable[1] or **CD-E** CD-ROM technology that enables users to store, access, and reuse compact disks in the same way that floppy disks can be used.

- Fingerspell: C-D-E

CD-Erasable[2] or **CD-E** (alternate sign)

- Fingerspell: C-D-E
- **erase** Rub the little-finger side of the right *S hand*, palm in, back and forth with a repeated movement on the palm of the left *open hand*, palm up.

CD-R See signs for CD-RECORDABLE[1,2].

CD-Recordable[1] or **CD-R** CD-ROM technology that enables users to write as well as read a compact disk.

- Fingerspell: C-D-R

CD-Recordable[2] or **CD-R** (alternate sign)

- Fingerspell: C-D-R
- **put-down** Touch the fingertips of the right *flattened O hand*, palm down, to the palm of the left *open hand*, palm up. Then slap the palm of the right *open hand* against the left palm.

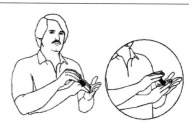

CD-ReWritable See sign for CD-RW.

CD-ROM Acronym for *Compact Disc–Read-Only Memory*. An optical disk capable of storing a large amount of data which cannot be erased or changed.

- Fingerspell: C-D-R-O-M

CD-RW or **CD-ReWritable** Acronym for *Compact Disc–Recordable-Writable*. An optical disk with the ability to read and write information just like a hard drive.

- Fingerspell: C-D-R-W

cell A single box in a spreadsheet application in which you can enter data.

- ■ Fingerspell: C-E-L-L

---

center A keyboard or mouse-click function that places the information being typed in the center of the line.

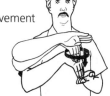

- ■ **center** Move the right *open hand*, palm down, in a circular movement over the left *open hand,* palm up, bending the right fingers as the hand moves and ending with the fingertips of the right *bent hand* touching the middle of the left palm.

---

central processing unit See sign for CPU.

---

chain 1. Linking of records by means of pointers in such a way that all like records are connected, the last record pointing to the first. 2. A set of operations that are performed sequentially. Same sign used for **chaining.**

- ■ **chain** Beginning with the index fingers and thumbs of both *F hands* intersecting in front of the left side of the chest, palms facing each other and the right hand above the left hand, release the fingers, flip the hands in reverse positions, and connect the fingers again with repeated alternating movements as the hands move across the front of the body from left to right.

---

chaining The process of linking a series of records or programs together sequentially. See sign for CHAIN.

---

channel A transmission path that connects two computers or connects peripheral devices to a computer. Same sign used for **branch.**

- ■ **channel** Slide the thumb side of the right *one hand*, palm down, from the heel to off the index finger of the left *5 hand*, palm right and fingers pointing forward. Repeat movement off the left ring finger.

---

character[1] Any letter, number, punctuation mark, or symbol that can be produced on-screen by the press of a key on the keyboard or, as with some special characters, a sequence of keys.

- ■ **character** Move the right *C hand,* palm left, in a small circle and then back against the left side of the chest.

---- [sign continues] -->

character

■ **letter** Touch the extended thumb of the right *10 hand* to the lips, palm in, and then move the thumb downward to touch the thumb of the left *10 hand* held in front of the chest, palm in.

character² (alternate sign)

■ **character** Move the right *C hand,* palm left, in a small circle and then back against the left side of the chest.

■ **symbol** With the index-finger side of the right *S hand*, palm forward, against the palm of the left *open hand* held in front of the chest, palm right and fingers pointing up, move both hands forward a short distance.

character set A defined list of letters, numbers, and symbols recognized by the computer.

■ **character** Move the right *C hand,* palm left, in a small circle and then back against the left side of the chest.

■ **group** Beginning with both *C hands* in front of the chest, palms facing each other, bring the hands away from each other in outward arcs while turning the palms in, ending with the little fingers near each other.

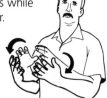

chart See sign for GRAPH.

chat room A virtual room, which is really a channel, where two or more users can communicate via computer.

■ **chat** Beginning with both *flattened C hands* near each side of the upper chest, palms facing each other, close the fingers and the thumbs together simultaneously with a double movement.

---- [sign continues] --->

- **room** Beginning with both *open hands* in front of each side of the chest, palms facing each other and fingers pointing forward, move the hands deliberately in opposite directions, ending with the left hand near the chest and the right hand several inches forward of the left hand, both palms facing in.

check See sign for VERIFY.

checkpoint A specified point at which a program can be interrupted as an aid in debugging.

- **check** Move the extended right index finger sharply upward off the upturned palm of the left *open hand*.

- **point** Move the extended right index finger forward to touch the left extended index finger held up in front of the chest.

chip[1] A small silicon wafer that contains a large amount of electronic circuitry used to perform various functions.

- **chip**[1] Touch the fingertips of the right *G hand* on the palm of the left *open hand* held in front of the chest. And then twist the right hand a half turn and touch the right fingers on the left palm again.

chip[2] (alternate sign)

- **chip**[2] Beginning with the fingers of both *G hands* touching in front of the chest, palms facing forward, bring the hands apart a short distance and pinch each thumb and index finger together.

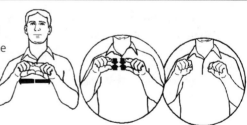

circuit An electric or electronic link between points.

- **circuit** Beginning with the little fingers of both *I hands* touching in front of the chest, palms facing each other, bring the hands apart to in front of each side of the chest, straight down, and then together again to touch in front of the chest.

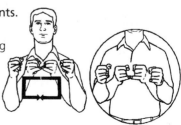

circuit board See signs for EXPANSION BOARD[1,2,3,4].

CISC (pronounced *sisk*) An acronym for *complex instruction set computer*. A central processing unit (CPU) that can recognize as many as 100 or more instructions and carry out most computations directly.
- Fingerspell: C-I-S-C

class A group having the same or similar characteristics.
- **group** Beginning with both *C hands* in front of the right side of the chest, palms facing each other, bring the hands away form each other in outward arcs while turning the palms in, ending with the little fingers near each other.

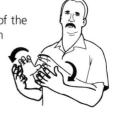

clear[1] A keyboard function that removes the contents from the display screen. Same sign used for **erase, purge.**
- **erase** rub the little-finger side of the right s hand, palm in, back and forth with a repeated movement on the palm of the left open hand, palm up.

clear[2] (alternate sign)
- **clean** Slide the palm of the right *open hand* from the heel to the fingers of the upturned palm of the left *open hand* with a repeated movement.

click To quickly press and release the button on a computer mouse to place the cursor at a particular position on a document or to make a selection.
- **click** Beginning with the right index finger pointing forward in front of the chest, bend the finger deliberately downward.

client In a computer network, any workstation that can use the resources of another, called a SERVER.
- **client** Move both *C hands*, palms facing each other, downward on each side of the chest.

clip art Artwork saved as a digital computer file that can be used to embellish documents.

- **clip** Beginning with the extended thumb, index finger, and middle finger of the right hand near the index-finger side of the left *open hand*, close the extended right fingers down on the left hand.

- **art** Move the extended right little finger with a wiggly movement down the palm of the left *open hand* from the fingers to the heel.

clipboard A portion of a computer's memory set aside to store data being transferred from one file or application to another. Same sign used for **Scrapbook**.

- **clip** Beginning with the extended thumb, index finger, and middle finger of the right hand near the index-finger side of the left *open hand*, close the extended right fingers down on the left hand.

- **board** Bring the little-finger side of the right *B hand*, palm left, sharply against the palm of the left *C hand* held in front of the chest, palm up.

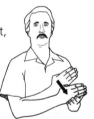

clock A device that regulates the rate at which instructions are executed and synchronizes all the various computer components.

- **time** Tap the bent index finger of the right *X hand*, palm down, with a double movement on the wrist of the downturned left hand.

- **clock-face** Hold both *modified C hands* in front of each side of the face, palms facing each other.

clock rate

clock rate See sign for CLOCK SPEED.

clock speed or **clock rate** The speed at which a microprocessor executes instructions; the faster the internal clock, the more instructions the computer can execute per second.

- **time** Tap the bent index finger of the right *X hand*, palm down, with a double movement on the wrist of the downturned left hand.

- **clock-face** Hold both *modified C hands* in front of each side of the face, palms facing each other.

- **fast** Beginning with the extended index fingers of both *one hands* pointing forward in front of the chest, pull the hands back toward the chest while changing to *S hands*.

clone A computer or software product that functions exactly like another computer or software product that is usually more expensive and has a more well-known brand name.

- **copy-it** Beginning with the fingertips of the right *5 hand* touching the extended left index finger held up in front of the chest, pull the right hand to the right while closing the fingers to the thumb forming a *flattened O* hand.

close 1. To finish a work session on a file and save it. 2. To exit an application and remove the window from the screen. Same sign used for: **abort, fatal error.**

- **close** Beginning with both *B hands* in front of each side of the chest, palms facing each other and fingers pointing forward, twist the wrists and bring them sharply toward each other until the index fingers touch, ending with palms facing down.

closed architecture See sign for PROPRIETARY.

closed bus system A bus system that comes with established ports into which cables attached to peripheral devices can be plugged.

- **close** Beginning with both *B hands* in front of each side of the chest, palms facing each other, twist the wrists and bring them sharply toward each other until the index fingers touch, ending with palms facing down.

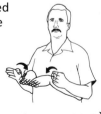

---- [sign continues] -->

- **bus** Beginning with the little-finger side of the right *B hand* touching the index-finger side of the left *B hand,* palms facing in opposite directions, move the right hand back toward the right shoulder.

- **system** Beginning with the index-finger sides of both *5 hands* touching in front of the chest, palms down, move the hands outward to in front of each shoulder and then straight down a short distance.

---

cluster A set of sectors that represents the minimum file size that can be created on a hard disk.
- Fingerspell: C-L-U-S-T-E-R

COBOL Acronym for *Common Business Oriented Language.* A programming language developed in the 1960s and used primarily for business applications for large mainframe computers.
- Fingerspell: C-O-B-O-L

---

code The process of translating instructions into computer language. See sign for WRITE.

---

cold boot Restarting a computer from a powered-down state.
- **cold** Shake both *A hands* with a slight movement in front of each side of the chest, palms facing each other.

- **kick** Bring the right *B hand* upward to strike the index-finger side of the right hand against the little-finger side of the left *open hand* held in front of the chest, palm angled up and fingers pointing forward.

---

collate To merge two or more sequenced data sets to produce a resulting data set that reflects the sequencing of the original sets.
- **collate** Beginning with the palms of both *open hands* together in front of the chest, fingers pointing forward, move the right hand in a series of double arcs to the right.

---

collection The process of gathering data from various sources and assembling it at one location.

- **collect** With a double movement, bring the little-finger side of the right *curved hand*, palm left, across the palm of the left *open hand*, palm up, from its fingertips to the heel while changing into an *S hand*.

column The vertical members of one line of an array. Same sign used for **field**.

- **column** Move the right *G hand*, palm forward, from in front of the right shoulder downward.

COM file An executable command file with a .COM extension, usually not exceeding 64K.

- Fingerspell: C-O-M
- **file** Slide the little-finger side of the right *B hand*, palm angled up, between the fingers of the left *5 hand*, palm facing in, first between the index and middle fingers and then between the ring and little fingers.

command 1. An instruction to a computer. 2. A keystroke, mouse action, voice input, or the like, directing the performance of a function.

- **order** Move the extended right index finger, palm left and finger pointing up, from in front of the mouth forward while turning the palm down, ending with the finger pointing forward.

command interpreter The portion of an operating system that executes a user's commands, as issued by typing commands directly onto a computer screen at the command line, pressing combinations of keys, or clicking icons with a mouse.

- **order** Move the extended right index finger, palm left and finger pointing up, from in front of the mouth forward while turning the palm down, ending with the finger pointing forward.

- **interpret** With the fingertips of both *F hands* touching in front of the chest, palms facing each other, twist the hands in opposite directions to reverse positions.

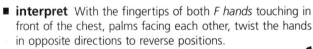

---- [sign continues] ---->

■ **person marker** Move both *open hands*, palms facing each other, downward along the sides of the body.

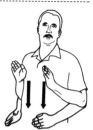

command-line The line on the display screen, in a nongraphical operating system, usually with a prompt indicating where a typed command is expected.

■ **order** Move the extended right index finger, palm left and finger pointing up, from in front of the mouth straight forward while turning the palm down, ending with the finger pointing forward.

■ **line** Beginning with the extended little fingers of both *I hands* touching in front of the chest, palms facing in, move both hands outward.

comment A brief explanation inserted into programs to describe what the program is supposed to do.

■ **say** Move the extended right index finger from in front of the mouth, palm facing in and finger pointing left, forward in a small arc.

■ **write** Slide the right *modified X hand*, palm facing left, from the base to the fingertips of the left *open hand*, palm facing right and fingers pointing forward.

Common Business Oriented Language See sign for COBOL.

common language See sign for UNIVERSAL LANGUAGE.

communicate To transmit information to a point of use. Related forms: **communicating, communication**.

■ **communication** Move both *C hands*, palms facing each other, forward and back from the mouth with an alternating movement.

communication link Hardware or software that permits the transfer of data between two links.

■ **communication** Move both *C hands*, palms facing each other, forward and back from the mouth with an alternating movement.

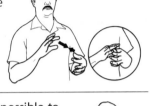

■ **connect** Beginning with both *curved 5 hands* in front of each side of the body, palms facing each other, bring the hands together while touching the thumb and index fingertips of each hand and intersecting with each other.

communications software Software that makes it possible to send and receive data, as over telephone lines through modems.

■ **communication** Move both *C hands*, palms facing each other, forward and back from the mouth with an alternating movement.

■ Fingerspell: S-W

Compact Disc-Read-Only-Memory See sign for CD-ROM.

compare To examine two numbers for identity and relative magnitude. Related form: **comparison**.

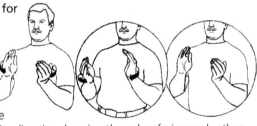

■ **compare** With both *curved hands* in front of each side of the chest, palms facing each other, alternately turn one hand and then the other toward the face while turning the other hand in the opposite direction, keeping the palms facing each other and the fingers pointing up.

compatible Referring to the ability of one device or program to work with another device or program. Related form: **compatibility**.

■ **compatible** Beginning with both *curved 5 hands* in front of each side of the chest, palms facing in, move the right hand to the left to mesh the fingers with the bent fingers of the left hand.

compilation time The time during which a source language program is translated into an object program that can be executed by a computer.

■ **convert**[1] With both *C hands* in front of the chest, thumbs touching, turn the right hand down and back up again.

---- [sign continues] -->

■ **time** Tap the bent index finger of the right *X hand*, palm down, with a double movement on the wrist of the downturned left hand.

compile To translate a computer program from the source code written by the programmer to object code that can be executed by a given computer. Same sign used for **conversion.** Related form: **compilation**.

■ **convert**[1] With both *C hands* in front of the chest, thumbs touching, turn the right hand down and back up again.

compiler A computer program whose purpose is to translate high-level computer programming language written by a programmer into machine language that can be executed by a computer.

■ **convert**[1] With both *C hands* in front of the chest, thumbs touching, turn the right hand down and back up again.

■ **person marker** Move both *open hands*, palms facing each other, downward along the sides of the body.

complex instruction set computer See sign for CISC.

compress To compact data for more efficient storage or transmission. Related form: **compression.** Compare EXPAND.

■ **compress** Beginning with both *5 hands* in front of the chest, right hand above the left hand and fingers pointing in opposite directions, bring the hands toward each other while squeezing the fingers together, ending with the little-finger side of the right *S hand* on top of the thumb side of the left *S hand*.

compute See sign for ARITHMETIC.

computer

computer[1] A programmable electronic machine for processing data at high speeds, including performing calculations, word processing, and database management.

- **computer**[1] Move the thumb side of the right *C hand*, palm left, from touching the lower part of the extended left arm upward to touch the upper arm.

computer[2] (alternate sign)

- **computer**[2] Move the right *C hand*, palm left, from the right side of the forehead forward with a circular movement.

computer[3] (alternate sign) [Used to indicate a reel-to-reel computer tape]

- **computer**[3] Beginning with both *C hands* in front of either side of the chest, palms facing forward, move both hands in simultaneous repeated circles going in opposite directions away from each other.

computer[4] (alternate sign) [Used to indicate a reel-to-reel computer tape]

- **computer**[4] beginning with both extended index fingers pointing forward in front of each side of the chest, palms facing down, move both fingers in simultaneous clockwise circles.

computer-aided design See sign for CAD.

computer graphics charts, graphs, diagrams, or pictures produced with the aid of a computer.

- **computer**[1] Move the thumb side of the right *C hand*, palm left, from touching the lower part of the extended left arm upward to touch the upper arm.

- **graphics** Move the little-finger side of the right *G hand*, palm in, with a wiggly movement across the palm of the left *open hand* held in front of the chest.

computer literacy A working knowledge of the way a computer operates and of at least some of the most popular software programs. Related form: **computer literate**.

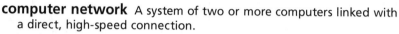

- **computer**[1] Move the thumb side of the right *C hand,* palm left, from touching the lower part of the extended left arm upward to touch the upper arm.
- Fingerspell: L-I-T-E-R-A-C-Y

computer network A system of two or more computers linked with a direct, high-speed connection.

- **computer**[1] Move the thumb side of the right *C hand,* palm left, from touching the lower part of the extended left arm upward to touch the upper arm.

- **network** Beginning with the bent middle fingers of both *5 hands* touching in front of the right side of the chest, right palm angled forward and left palm facing in, twist both wrists and touch again in front of the left side of the chest, ending with the right palm facing in and left palm angled forward.

concatenate To link together. You can, for example, concatenate strings of characters to form a word or wordlike unit or a group of files to form a single file.

- **connect** Beginning with both *curved 5 hands* in front of each side of the body, palms facing each other, bring the hands together while touching the thumb and index fingertips of each hand and intersecting with each other.

concurrent[1] or **simultaneous** Pertaining to the occurrence of two or more events or activities within the same specified interval of time.

- **time** Tap the bent index finger of the right *X hand*, palm down, with a double movement on the wrist of the downturned left hand.

- **still** Beginning with both *Y hands* in front of each side of the chest, palms facing down, move the hands downward and forward with simultaneous movements.

concurrent² or **simultaneous** (alternate sign)

- **same** Tap the sides of the both extended index fingers, palms facing down, together in front of the chest.

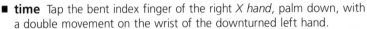

- **time** Tap the bent index finger of the right *X hand*, palm down, with a double movement on the wrist of the downturned left hand.

condition¹ or **decision** A programming construct in which one set of instructions is executed if a condition is true, and a different set of instructions is executed if the condition is false.

- **decide** Move the extended right index finger from the right side of the forehead, palm left, down in front of the chest while changing into an *F hand*, ending with both *F hands* moving downward in front of the body, palms facing each other.

condition² or **decision** (alternate sign)

- **condition** Beginning with the right *C hand*, palm left, near the extended left index finger, palm right, move the right hand in a circle forward and around the left finger.

configuration 1. The way that a computer and peripherals in a system are connected and programmed to function together. 2. The basic attributes of an application or device, often under control of the user, such as how an application appears on screen or the direction of output to a certain type of printer. Related form: **configure**.

- Fingerspell: C-O-N-F-I-G

configuration files A file made by the user during installation of an application program, which stores the choices made by the user at each step of the installation and makes them available each time the program starts.

- Fingerspell: C-O-N-F-I-G
- **file** Slide the little-finger side of the right *B hand*, palm angled up, between the fingers of the left *5 hand*, palm facing in, first between the index and middle fingers and then between the middle and ring fingers.

connect To attach one device to another by plugging into a port or interface. Same sign used for link.

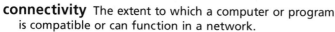

- **connect-connect** Beginning with both *curved 5 hands* in front of the left side of the body, palms facing each other, bring the hands together while touching the thumb and index fingertips of each hand and intersecting with each other. Repeat in front of the right side of the body.

connectivity The extent to which a computer or program is compatible or can function in a network.

- **connect** Beginning with both *curved 5 hands* in front of each side of the body, palms facing each other, bring the hands together while touching the thumb and index fingertips of each hand and intersecting with each other.

- **can** Move both *S hands,* palms facing down, downward simultaneously with a double movement in front of each side of the body.

connector The part of a cable that plugs into a port or interface to connect one device to another.

- **connect** Beginning with both *curved 5 hands* in front of each side of the body, palms facing each other, bring the hands together while touching the thumb and index fingertips of each hand and intersecting with each other.

- **person marker** Move both *open hands*, palms facing each other, downward along the sides of the body.

connect time The amount of time that a user is on line with a remote service provider.

- **connect** Beginning with both *curved 5 hands* in front of each side of the body, palms facing each other, bring the hands together while touching the thumb and index fingertips of each hand and intersecting with each other.

---- [sign continues] --→

connect time

- **time** Tap the bent index finger of the right *X hand*, palm down, with a double movement on the wrist of the downturned left hand.

---

console or **front panel** The combination of a computer's display monitor and keyboard.

- **panel** Beginning with both extended index fingers touching in front of the chest, palms facing forward, move the hands outward to each side of the chest and then down and back together in front of the chest.

- **type** Wiggle the fingers of both *5 hands* in front of the body, palms facing down.

---

constant In programming, a value that never changes, as contrasted with a *variable*, which is a value that changes.

- **constant** Beginning with the right *open hand* in front of the right shoulder, palm facing down and fingers pointing forward, move the hand straight forward in a slow movement.

---

content Information contained in a file as entered by the user.

- **meat** With the bent index finger and thumb of the right *5 hand*, palm down, grasp the fleshy part of the left *open hand* near the thumb, palm right and fingers pointing forward, and shake the hands with a small repeated movement.

Control key Often abbreviated *Ctrl*. A keyboard key that is used in conjunction with other keys to modify their actions or to execute commands.

- **control** Beginning with both *modified X hands* in front of each side of the body, right hand forward of the left hand and palms facing each other, move the hands forward and back with a repeated movement.

---- [sign continues] --->

■ **key** Push the extended thumb of the right *10 hand* downward a short distance in front of the right side of the body.

---

controller See signs for MOTHERBOARD[1,2].

---

control module The top box in a structure chart used to indicate tasks a program must accomplish.

■ **control** Beginning with both *modified X hands* in front of each side of the body, right hand forward of the left hand and palms facing each other, move the hands forward and back with a repeated movement.

■ Fingerspell: M-O-D-U-L-E

Control Program for Microcomputers See sign for CP/M.

---

control unit The portion of the central processing unit that directs the step-by-step operation of the entire computing system.

■ **control** Beginning with both *modified X hands* in front of each side of the body, right hand forward of the left hand and palms facing each other, move the hands forward and back with a repeated movement.

■ Fingerspell: U-N-I-T

---

conversational Pertaining to a program that carries on a conversation with the user, alternately accepting input, and then responding to the input quickly enough for the user to maintain the thought process. Same sign used for **talk**.

■ **talk** Beginning with both extended index fingers pointing up in front of the mouth, right hand closer to the mouth than the left hand and palms facing each other, move the hands forward and back with an alternating movement.

---

conversational language Computer programming language commands that approximate real language, such as BASIC.

■ **talk** Beginning with both extended index fingers pointing up in front of the mouth, right hand closer to the mouth than the left hand and palms facing each other, move the hands forward and back with an alternating movement.

■ **language** Beginning with the thumbs of both *L hands* near each other in front of the chest, palms angled down, bring the hands outward with a wavy movement to in front of each side of the chest.

conversion

conversion[1] The changing of a computer data file format to adapt it for a different use, as from a word processing document to a spreadsheet, or to make it compatible with another program.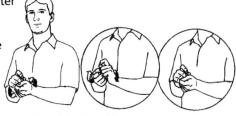

- **convert**[2] Beginning with the palms of both *modified X hands* together, twist the hands in opposite directions to reverse positions, and then back again to the original position.

conversion[2] See sign for COMPILE.

cookie Information about a user, saved as a small file on a hard drive by a Web page or server, that provides assistance next time that Web page or server is visited.

- Fingerspell: C-O-O-K-I-E

coprocessor An auxiliary chip that augments the functions of the central processing unit.

- Fingerspell: C-O

- **process** Beginning with both *open hands* in front of the body, palms facing in, left fingers pointing right and right fingers pointing left, and the left hand closer to the chest than the right hand, move the left over the right hand and then the right over the left hand in an alternating movement.

- **person marker** Move both *open hands*, palms facing each other, downward along the sides of the body.

copy or **duplicate** 1. To make a duplicate of a file in order to move or copy it from one directory (or folder) to another, from a disk to a hard drive, from a hard drive to a removable disk, etc. 2. To make a duplicate of text or graphics for insertion elsewhere in the document. 3. An exact reproduction of text or graphics.

- **copy**[1] Move the fingers of the right *curved hand,* from touching the palm of the left *open hand,* while closing the right fingers and thumb forming a *flattened O hand*. The noun is formed in the same way except with a double movement.

copyprotected software Software protected by programming techniques that do not allow unauthorized duplication. See sign for COPYRIGHTED SOFTWARE.

copyrighted software Software legally protected against copying or being used without paying for it. Same sign used for: **copy-protected software**.

- **can't** Bring the extended index finger of the right *one hand* downward, hitting the extended index finger of the left *one hand* as it moves.

- **copy**[1] Move the fingers of the right *curved hand* from touching the palm of the left *open hand* while closing the right fingers and thumb forming a *flattened O hand*.

- Fingerspell: S-W

---

count The successive increase or decrease of the cumulative total of the number of times that an event occurs.

- **count** Move the fingertips of the right *F hand*, palm down, across the upturned palm of the left *open hand* from the heel to the fingers with a repeated movement.

CP/M Acronym for *Control Program for Microcomputers*. An operating system that predated DOS, popular in the 1970s.

- Fingerspell: C-P-M

CPU, microprocessor, or **processor** Abbreviation of *central processing unit* and pronounced as separate letters. The CPU is the brains of a computer where most calculations take place.

- Fingerspell: C-P-U

---

crack An illegal attempt to break into a secure computer system.

- Fingerspell: C-R-A-C-K

---

cracker Someone who breaks into a computer system electronically, often to steal information or disrupt the system.

- Fingerspell: C-R-A-C-K-E-R

---

crash[1] or **bomb** 1. A situation in which the computer ceases to process or respond to commands from the keyboard or mouse and must be restarted, often with an accompanying loss of data. 2. A disk failure caused by the read/write head striking the disk.

- **crash** Beginning with the right *5 hand* near the right side of the chest, palm down and fingers pointing forward, move the hand deliberately forward to hit against the palm of the left *open hand*, bending the right fingers as it hits.

crash[2] or **bomb** (alternate sign)

- **break down** [Indicates things crumbling down] Beginning with the fingertips of both *curved 5 hands* touching in front of the chest, palms facing each other, allow the fingers to loosely drop, ending with the palms facing down.

create[1] 1. To make a new file on a disk, as opposed to modifying an existing file. 2. To define the fields for a database record, specifying field name, length, field type, and so on.

- **invent** Move the index-finger side of the right *4 hand*, palm left, from the forehead upward and forward in an arc.

create[2] (alternate sign)

- **make** Beginning with the little-finger side of the right *S hand* on the index-finger side of the left *S hand*, separate the hands slightly, twist the wrists in opposite directions, and touch the hands together again.

critical path The path through a network that defines the shortest possible time in which the entire project can be completed.

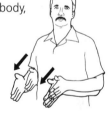

- **goal** Move the extended right index finger from touching the right side of the forehead, palm down, forward to point to the extended left index finger held in front of the face.

- **path** Move both *open hands* from in front of each side of the body, palms facing each other, forward with a parallel movement.

crop In desktop publishing, to trim off unwanted parts of a picture or graphic image. Same sign used for **cut**.

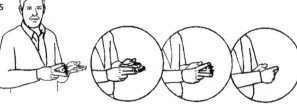

- **cut** Move the right *V hand*, palm left, around the fingertips of the left *open hand*, palm up, while opening and closing the right index and middle fingers with a repeated movement as the hand moves.

crop marks[1] In desktop publishing, marks that
are placed on each page to indicate proper
alignment for the printer.

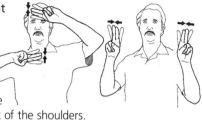

- **cut-cut**[1] With the right *V hand* in front
of the face and the left *V hand* in front
of the chest, both palms facing forward and
fingers pointing in opposite directions, close the
extended fingers of both hands. Repeat in front of the shoulders.

crop marks[2] (alternate sign)

- **cut-cut**[2] With both *V hands* near each
side of the head, palms facing back and
fingers pointing toward the head, twist both
hands forward, ending with the fingers
pointing forward. Repeat near each side of
the body.

crosshairs On an input device, two intersecting
lines—one horizontal and one vertical—whose
intersection marks the active cursor position of
a graphics system.

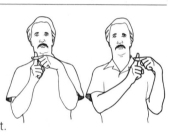

- **cross-hairs** Bring the left extended index finger,
pointing right, inward to cross the extended right
index finger, pointing up in front of the right side of
the chest. Repeat in front of the left side of the chest.

cross-platform Describing a program
designed for use on more than one kind of
hardware or operating system, as on both PC
and Apple processors or on Windows and
Unix.

- **across** Push the little-finger side of the
right *B hand,* palm left, across the back of
the left *B hand,* held in front of the left side
of the chest, palm down. Repeat in front of the right side of the chest.

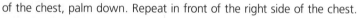

- **floor** Beginning with the index-finger side of both *B hands* touching
in front of the body, palms facing down and fingers pointing
forward, move the hands apart to each side.

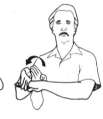

CRT See sign for DISPLAY SCREEN.

CSO name server A searchable white-pages listing of real names and associated E-mail addresses, usually reached via gopher. See sign for NAME SERVER.

Ctrl See sign for CONTROL KEY.

cursor

cursor or **prompt** The dash, block, or other symbol on a monitor screen that marks the insertion point for text or graphics, or the location where the next action is to take place.

- **cursor** Beginning with the right *modified X hand* in front of the right shoulder, palm angled forward, move the right hand upward and forward with a jagged movement.

---

cursor control keys See sign for NAVIGATION KEYS.

---

customer support See sign for SUPPORT SERVICES.

---

cut To remove text or graphics from a document. See sign for CROP.

---

cut and paste The process of deleting text or graphics and placing the deleted material in another location in the same or another document.

- **cut** Move the right *V hand*, palm left, across the fingertips of the left *open hand*, palm down, while opening and closing the right index and middle fingers with a repeated movement as the hand moves.

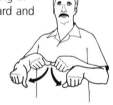

- **and** Move the right *5 hand*, palm in and fingers pointing left, from in front of the left side of the body to the right while closing the fingers to a *flattened O hand*.

- **paste-up** Beginning with the thumbs of both *10 hands* touching in front of the chest, palms facing down, bring the hands downward and apart with a double movement by twisting the wrists.

---

cut off See sign for TRUNCATE.

---

cyberphobia An extreme and irrational fear of computers.

- Fingerspell: C-Y-B-E-R-P-H-O-B-I-A
- **afraid** Beginning with both *A hands* in front of each side of the chest, spread the fingers open with a quick movement, forming *5 hands*, palms facing in and fingers pointing toward each other.

---- [sign continues] -->

- **computer**[1] Move the thumb side of the right *C hand*, palm left, from touching the lower part of the extended left arm upward to touch the upper arm.

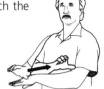

Cyberspace The electronic domain where online communications take place via international networks, bulletin board systems, etc.

- Fingerspell: C-Y-B-E-R-S-P-A-C-E

cycle or **pass** A periodic sequence of events occurring when information is transferred to or from a storage device or a computer.

- **cycle** Move the extended right index finger in a circle around the opening formed by the left *modified C hand* held in front of the left side of the body, palm down and fingers pointing down.

cylinder or **drum** All of the tracks that occupy a specific position one above the other in a stack of computer storage disks that make up the hard disk.

- **cylinder** Move both *C hands*, palms facing each other, from in front of each side of the waist upward in front of the chest.

D-to-A See sign for DIGITAL-TO-ANALOG.

daisy chain **1.** To connect a series of peripherals to a computer system, one after another. **2.** In word processing to print several documents one after another.

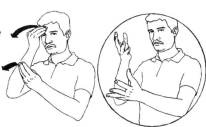

- Fingerspell: D-A-I-S-Y

- **chain** Beginning with the index fingers and thumbs of both *F hands* intersecting in front of the left side of the chest, palms facing each other and the right hand above the left hand, release the fingers, flip the hands in reverse positions, and connect the fingers again with repeated alternating movements as the hands move across the front of the body from left to right.

data[1] Information that is formatted in a special way. In the computer world, data consists of text, numbers, etc., digitized so as to be readable and manipulable electronically.

- Fingerspell: D-A-T-A

data[2] or **information** (alternate sign)

- **inform** Beginning with the fingertips of the right *flattened O hand* near the forehead and the left *flattened O hand* in front of the chest, move both hands forward while opening into *5 hands*, palms facing up.

database A collection of information organized in such a way that a computer program can quickly select desired pieces of data. Traditional databases are organized by *fields, records,* and *files.*

- Fingerspell: D-B

database files A collection of data records.

- Fingerspell: D-A-T-A

- **file** Slide the little-finger side of the right *B hand,* palm angled up, between the fingers of the left *5 hand,* palm facing in, first between the index and middle fingers and then between the middle and ring fingers.

data compression Storing data in a format that requires less space than usual.

- Fingerspell: D-A-T-A

- **compress** Beginning with both *5 hands* in front of the chest, right hand above the left hand and fingers pointing in opposite directions, bring the hands toward each other while squeezing the fingers together, ending with the little-finger side of the right *S hand* on top of the thumb side of the left *S hand*.

data entry The process of entering or updating data in a computer database.

- Fingerspell: D-A-T-A

- **enter** Move the back of the right *open hand* forward in a down-ward arc under the palm of the left *open hand*, both palms down.

data processing A class of programs that organize and manipulate data as by sorting, reformatting, or creating a report. Usually data processing involves large amounts of numeric data as contrasted with text, which is manipulated in word processing.

- Fingerspell: D-A-T-A

- **process** Beginning with both *open hands* in front of the body, palms facing in, left fingers pointing right and right fingers pointing left, and the left hand closer to the chest than the right hand, move the left over the right hand and then the right over the left hand in an alternating movement.

deadlock An unresolved contention for the use of a resource.

- **stuck** Move the fingertips of the right *V hand*, palm down, against the throat with a deliberate movement.

debug[1] To find and correct errors in a computer program or the operation of a piece of equipment.

- Fingerspell: D-B

debug[2] (alternate sign)

- **delete** Beginning with the index finger of the right *modified X hand*, palm in, touching the extended left index finger held up in front of the chest, palm right and finger pointing up, move the right hand upward to the right while flicking the thumb upward.

---- [sign continues] --➤

debug

- **insect** With the extended thumb of the right *3 hand* on the nose, palm left, bend the extended index and middle fingers with a double movement.

decimal[1], decimal number, or **base ten** A value greater than 9 represented in base 10, such as 50, 483, 1,222, etc.

- **base + ten** Move the right *B hand*, palm forward and fingers pointing up, to the right under the palm of the left *open hand* held across the chest, while changing into a *10 hand*.

decimal[2], decimal point, or **dot** A fraction based on the number 10, usually written with a dot (decimal point) before the numerator.

- **period** With the right index finger and thumb pinched together, palm forward, push the right hand forward a short distance.

decimal number See sign for DECIMAL[1].

decimal point See sign for DECIMAL[2].

decision See signs for CONDITION[1,2].

decision symbol A diamond-shaped flowcharting symbol that is used to indicate a choice or a branching in the information processing path.

- **decide** Move the extended right index finger from the right side of the forehead, palm left, down in front of the chest while changing into an *F hand*, ending with both *F hands* moving downward in front of the body, palms facing each other.

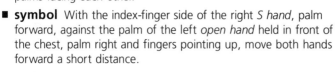

- **symbol** With the index-finger side of the right *S hand*, palm forward, against the palm of the left *open hand* held in front of the chest, palm right and fingers pointing up, move both hands forward a short distance.

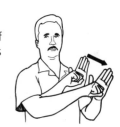

decode To translate or determine the meaning of coded information. Compare ENCODE.

- **decode** Beginning with the fingertips of both *D hands* touching in front of the chest, palms facing each other, twist the hands in opposite directions with a double movement.

---

decoder Special software that translates encoded messages back to real text that a person can understand.

- **decoder** Beginning with the index-finger sides of both *D hands* touching in front of the chest, palms forward, move the hands apart to each side with a double movement.

---

dedicated Pertaining to programs, equipment, or procedures set aside for a specific purpose, such as *dedicated computer, dedicated line, dedicated network, dedicated server*.

- **specialize** Slide the extended right index finger, palm in, from the base to the fingertip of the index finger of the left *B hand*, palm in.

- **reserve** Move the right *S hand*, palm down, in a small circle and then down to the back of the left *A hand*, palm down in front of the chest.

---

default A value or setting that a computer or program automatically selects if a substitute is not specified, such as *default configuration, default directory*.

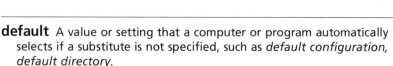

- **take** Beginning with both *curved 5 hands* in front of each side of the body, palms facing down, move the hands upward toward the body while changing into *S hands*.

---

default directory The directory on the hard disk that the computer or a software program uses to perform commands if it isn't given specific instructions to use another directory. See sign for ROOT DIRECTORY.

---

default values The assigned quantity for a device or program that is set by the manufacturer.

- **start** Beginning with the extended right index finger, palm down, inserted between the index and middle fingers of the left *open hand*, palm right and fingers pointing forward, twist the right hand, ending with palm anged forward.

---- [sign continues] -->

default values

- **value** Beginning with the index fingers of both *V hands* touching in front of the chest, palms facing down, move the hands outward and upward in arcs, ending with the index fingers touching and the palms facing forward.

deferred The passing of control to a subroutine at a time determined by an asynchronous event rather than at a predictable time.

- **postpone** Beginning with both *F hands* in front of the body, palms facing each other and the left hand nearer the body then the right, move both hands forward in small arcs.

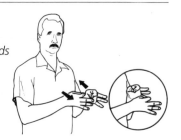

define or **describe** To set a value for a symbol or variable. Related forms: **definition, description**.

- **describe** Beginning with the fingers of both *F hands* in front of the chest, palms facing each other and index fingers pointing forward, move the hands forward and back with an alternating movement.

degradation A decline in the performance of a computer system as it continues to operate.

- **decline** Touch the little-finger side of the right *open hand,* palm in, first near the shoulder, then near the elbow, and finally near the wrist of the extended left arm.

Del See sign for DELETE KEY.

delete or **remove** To erase or cancel text or a file. To remove or eliminate data or a file. Same sign used for **zap** (*slang*).

- **delete** Beginning with the index finger of the right *modified X hand,* palm in, touching the extended left index finger held up in front of the chest, palm right and finger pointing up, move the right hand upward to the right while flicking the thumb upward.

descriptor

Delete key or **Del** A keyboard key that eliminates either the character to the left or to the right of the cursor, depending on the program.

- **delete** Beginning with the index finger of the right *modified X hand*, palm in, touching the extended left index finger held up in front of the chest, palm right and finger pointing up, move the right hand upward to the right while flicking the thumb upward.

- **key** Push the extended thumb of the right *10 hand* downward a short distance in front of the right side of the body.

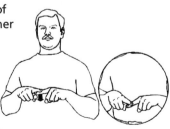

delimit To fix the limits of something, such as to establish maximum and minimum limits of a specific variable.

- **limit** Beginning with both *bent hands* in front of the chest, right hand above the left hand and both palms facing down, move both hands forward simultaneously.

density The amount of information that can be stored in a given physical space.

- **density** Shake the right *D hand*, palm forward, in front of the chest.

dependency A relationship where the execution of one job has to have been completed before another can begin.

- **depend** With the extended right index finger across the extended left index finger, both palms facing down, move both fingers down slightly with a double movement.

describe See sign for DEFINE.

descriptor See sign for KEYWORD.

deselect To remove the blocking or highlight from a selected item.

- **not** Bring the extended thumb of the right *10 hand* from under the chin, palm left, forward with a deliberate movement.

- **select** Beginning with the thumb side of the right *5 hand*, palm forward, near the left *open hand* palm right and fingers pointing up, pull the right hand back to touch the left palm while pinching the index finger and thumb together.

design or **diagram** 1. In a hardware system, the cycle of proto-typing, test, and development. 2. In a software system, the cycle of problem description, algorithm development, coding, program debugging, and documentation.

- **design** Move the fingertips of the right *D hand*, palm left, down the palm of the left *open hand* with a wavy movement.

desktop The background that appears in graphical operating systems containing icons permitting shortcuts to programs.

- Fingerspell: D-E-S-K-T-O-P

desktop computer[1]**, personal computer,** or **PC** A computer that is small enough to sit on top of or underneath a desk but too large to be easily portable; designed for individual use at home or in a business.

- Fingerspell: P-C

desktop computer[2]**, personal computer,** or **PC** (alternate sign)

- **personal** Move the right *P hand*, palm down, in a small double circle on the left side of the chest with a double movement.

- **computer**[1] Move the thumb side of the right *C hand*, palm left, from touching the lower part of the extended left arm upward to touch the upper arm.

desktop publishing The use of a computer to lay out pages containing text and graphics to produce high-quality newsletters, brochures, books, and other publications.

- **table** Beginning with the bent arms of both *open hands* across the chest, right arm above the left arm, move the right arm down with a short double movement.

- **print** Beginning with the thumb of the right *G hand* on the heel of the left *open hand*, tap the right index finger down to the thumb with a double movement.

destination or **target** A data file, directory or folder, computer, or peripheral device to which data is being transmitted. Compare with SOURCE.

- **goal** Move the extended right index finger from touching the right side of the forehead, palm down, forward to point to the extended left index finger held in front of the face.

destructive operation A process of reading or writing data that erases the data that was stored previously in the receiving storage location.

- **destroy** Beginning with both *curved 5 hands* in front of the chest, right hand over the left, right palm facing down and left palm facing up, bring the right hand in a circular movement over the left. Then close both hands into *A hands* and bring the knuckles of the right hand past the left knuckles as the right hand moves forward to the right with a deliberate movement.

detail A small section of a larger file or graphics picture.

- **describe** Beginning with the fingers of both *F hands* in front of the chest, palms facing each other and index fingers pointing forward, move the hands forward and back with an alternating movement.

- **deep** Move the extended right index finger, palm down, downward from the fingertips past the heel of the left *open hand,* palm right and fingers pointing up.

develop or **program** To prepare a program by writing a series of instructions that will cause a computer to process data.

- **develop** Move the fingertips of the right *D hand*, palm left, upward from the heel to the fingers of the left *open hand*, fingers pointing up and palm facing right.

device[1], **equipment,** or **hardware** Any machine or component that attaches to a computer such as disk drives, modems, printers, etc.

- **equipment** Move the right *E hand*, palm up, from in front of the middle of the body to the right in a double arc.

device[2], **equipment,** or **hardware** (alternate sign)

- **machine** With the fingers of both *curved 5 hands* loosely meshed together, palms facing in, move the hands up and down in front of the chest with a repeated movement.

diagnosis or **diagnostics** The process of isolating malfunctions in computing equipment and of detecting mistakes in programs and systems.

- **diagnose** Bring the right *D hand*, palm left and index finger pointing up, from near the right cheek, downward to the palm of the left *open hand* and then across the left palm off the fingertips.

diagram See sign for DESIGN.

dialog box A pane that appears on screen as part of a program to furnish instructions or information, or to request user input.

- **talk** Beginning with both extended index fingers pointing up in front of the mouth, right hand closer to the mouth than the left hand and palms facing each other, move the hands forward and back with an alternating movement.

- **square** Beginning with both extended index fingers side by side in front of the chest, palms facing down and fingers pointing forward, bring the hands apart to in front of each shoulder, then straight down, and finally back together again in front of the lower chest.

dial-up access The use of a personal computer and a modem to connect to a network or to the Internet. Compare BROADBAND.

- **telephone** Bring the knuckles of the right *Y hand* in to touch the lower right cheek, holding the right thumb near the right ear and the little finger in front of the mouth.

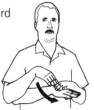

- **enter** Move the back of the right *open hand* forward in a downward arc under the palm of the left *open hand*, both palms down.

dictionary A collection of words arranged alphabetically and usually defined. See sign for DIRECTORY.

dictionary program or **spell-check program** A program to find and correct misspelled words in documents, often used with word processing systems.

- **spell** Move the right *5 hand*, palm down, from in front of the chest to the right while wiggling the fingers.

- **check** Move the extended right index finger sharply upward off the upturned palm of the left *open hand*.

- **program** Move the middle finger of the right *P hand*, palm left, from the fingertips to the base of the left *open hand*, palm right and fingers pointing up. Repeat the movement on the back side of the left hand.

digit or **number** One of the symbols of a numbering system that is used to designate a quantity. Same sign used for **integer**.

- **number** Beginning with the fingertips of both *flattened O hands* touching, palms facing in opposite directions, bring the hands apart slightly while twisting the wrists in opposite directions and touch the fingertips again.

digital

digital[1] Relating to the computer technology wherein all information is encoded as bits of 1s or 0s that represent on or off states. Related form: **digitize**.

- **to** Move the extended right index finger, palm down and finger pointing forward, a short distance forward to meet the extended left index finger held up in front of the chest, palm in.

- **number** Beginning with the fingertips of both *flattened O hands* touching, palms facing in opposite directions, bring the hands apart slightly while twisting the wrists in opposite directions and touch the fingertips again.

---

digital[2] Relating to information recorded according to a system of numbers.

- **to** Move the extended right index finger, palm down and finger pointing forward, a short distance forward to meet the extended left index finger held up in front of the chest, palm in.

- **number** Beginning with the fingertips of both *flattened O hands* touching, palms facing in opposite directions, bring the hands apart slightly while twisting the wrists in opposite directions and touch the fingertips again.

- **group** Beginning with both *C hands* in front of the right side of the chest, palms facing each other, bring the hands away from each other in outward arcs while turning the palms in, ending with the little fingers near each other.

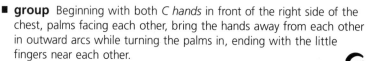

---

digital subscriber line See sign for DSL.

---

digital-to-analog or **D-to-A** The conversion of discrete digital numbers to continuous analog signals.

- **digital-to-analog** Touch the heel of the right *D hand*, palm forward, to the thumb of the left *5 hand*, palm in. Then, touch the heel of the right *A hand*, palm forward, to the index finger of the left *5 hand*, palm in.

digitizing The process of converting graphic representations, such as pictures and drawings, into digital data that can be processed by a computer.

- **change**[2] With the palm side of both *S hands* facing each other, twist the wrists in opposite directions in order to reverse positions.

- **to** Move the extended right index finger, palm down and finger pointing forward, a short distance forward to meet the extended left index finger held up in front of the chest, palm in.

- **number** Beginning with the fingertips of both *flattened O hands* touching, palms facing in opposite directions, bring the hands apart slightly while twisting the wrists in opposite directions and touch the fingertips again.

direct access or **random access** The process of storing and retrieving data from a storage device so that surrounding data need not be scanned to locate the desired data. Compare SEQUENTIAL ACCESS.

- **goal** Move the extended right index finger from touching the right side of the forehead, palm down, forward to point to the extended left index finger held in front of the face.

- **enter** Move the back of the right *open hand* forward in a downward arc under the palm of the left *open hand*, both palms down.

direct access processing See sign for RANDOM PROCESSING.

directory or **folder** A file on a disk containing other directories (or *subdirectories*) and other files, listing them by name. Same sign used for **dictionary**.

- **directory** Move the fingertips of the right *D hand*, palm down, across the palm of the left *open hand* with a double upward movement.

disable To remove or inhibit the normal capability of a device. Compare with ENABLE.

- **prevent** With the little-finger side of the right *B hand* against the index-finger side of the left *B hand*, palms facing in opposite directions, move the hands forward a short distance.

disconnect To break one's connection to the Internet voluntarily or have it broken by one's on-line service provider, as when one has not been actively using the connection for a period of time or when one has reached the time limit allowed by the provider.

- **disconnect** Beginning with the thumb and index fingertips of each hand intersecting with each other, palms facing each other and right hand nearer the chest than the left hand, release the fingers and pull the left hand forward and the right hand back toward the right shoulder.

disk¹, diskette, floppy disk, or **volume** A round magnetic device for storing information and programs accessible by a computer.

- **disk** Move the fingertips of the right *D hand,* palm facing down and index finger pointing forward, in a double circle on the upturned left *open hand.*

disk², diskette, floppy disk, or **volume** (alternate sign)

- **floppy** With both *flattened O hands* near each other in front of the chest, palms facing in, bend the wrists to move the hands forward and back with an alternating repeated movement.

- **disk** Move the fingertips of the right *D hand,* palm facing down and index finger pointing forward, in a double circle on the upturned left *open hand.*

disk compression A technique for compacting data on a disk for more efficient storage.

- **disk** Move the fingertips of the right *D hand,* palm facing down and index finger pointing forward, in a double circle on the upturned left *open hand.*

---- [sign continues] --→

■ **compress** Beginning with both *5 hands* in front of the chest, right hand above the left hand and fingers pointing in opposite directions, bring the hands toward each other while squeezing the fingers together, ending with the little-finger side of the right *S hand* on top of the thumb side of the left *S hand*.

disk drive or **drive** A machine that contains the mechanism that spins the disk, and that reads or writes to it.

■ **disk** Move the fingertips of the right *D hand*, palm facing down and index finger pointing forward, in a double circle on the upturned left *open hand*.

■ Fingerspell: D-R-I-V-E

diskette See signs for DISK[1,2].

Disk Operating System See sign for DOS.

display The physical representation of data on a screen.

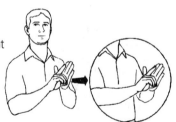

■ **display** Beginning with the thumb side of the right *D hand*, palm forward, against the palm of the left *open hand*, palm right, move both hands forward from the chest.

display screen, cathode ray tube, CRT, flat-panel screen, or **screen** The TV-like display screen, including the box surrounding it, that permits viewing programs and data and facilitates the user's interaction with the computer.

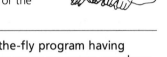

■ **screen** Beginning with both extended index fingers side by side in front of the chest, palms facing down and fingers pointing forward, bring the hands apart to in front of each shoulder, then straight down, and finally back together again in front of the lower chest.

DLL Abbreviation for *Dynamic Link Library*. **1.** An on-the-fly program having files that contain commonly used routines that two or more programs can share. **2.** The extension for a DLL file.

■ Fingerspell: D-L-L

DOC 1. An abbreviation for *document*. **2.** The extension for a DOC file, which is a document file; often used by word processors, especially Microsoft Word.

■ Fingerspell: D-O-C

document

document[1] A text file, usually one produced by a word processor.

- **document** Move the fingers of the right *D hand*, palm left, from the heel to off the fingers of the palm of the left *open hand*, palm right, with a double movement.

document[2] See sign for DOC.

documentation Instructions for using a computer device or program, most commonly found in a manual, but sometimes located on-line. Compare MANUAL.

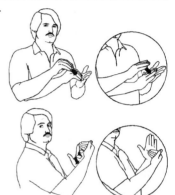

- **put-down** Touch the fingertips of the right *flattened O hand*, palm down, to the palm of the left *open hand*, palm up. Then slap the palm of the right *open hand* against the left palm.

- **list**[1] Touch the little-finger side of the right *bent hand*, palm in, from the fingertips of the left *open hand* down the left forearm.

domain or **domain name** A name used for identifying an organization on an Internet web site, the suffix of which specifies the type of organization, such as *gov* for government, *edu* for educational institution, or the geographic location, such as *uk* for the United Kingdom and *ca* for Canada.

- **identify** Tap the thumb side of the right *I hand*, palm left, with a double movement against the left *open hand* held in front of the chest, palm forward and fingers pointing up.

- **name** Tap the middle-finger side of the right *H hand* across the index-finger side of the left *H hand* with a double movement.

domain name See sign for DOMAIN.

domain name server See sign for NAME SERVER.

DOS Acronym for *Disk Operating System*, a proprietary program that controls all of the basic operations of a computer.

- Fingerspell: D-O-S

DOS command Any of the instructions typed at a DOS prompt that tells the computer what to do.

- Fingerspell: D-O-S

---- [sign continues] --->

76

■ **order** Move the extended right index finger, palm left and finger pointing up, from in front of the mouth straight forward while turning the palm down, ending with the finger pointing forward.

dot See sign for DECIMAL².

dot-com *Slang.* A company or individual who does business solely through order taking and processing as a result of advertising on a Web site, e.g., *a dot-com business.*

■ **period** With the right index finger and thumb pinched together, palm forward, push the right hand forward a short distance.

■ Fingerspell: C-O-M

dot-matrix printer An impact printer that forms letters and graphics by hammering the ends of pins against a ribbon in a pattern (matrix) of dots.

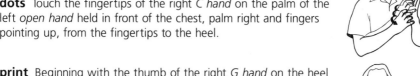

■ **dots** Touch the fingertips of the right *C hand* on the palm of the left *open hand* held in front of the chest, palm right and fingers pointing up, from the fingertips to the heel.

■ **print** Beginning with the thumb of the right *G hand* on the heel of the left *open hand*, tap the right index finger down to the thumb with a double movement.

■ **person marker** Move both *open hands*, palms facing each other, downward along the sides of the body.

dot pitch The diagonal distance between pixels on a display screen. The lower the dot pitch, the higher the resolution and quality of the image.

■ **dots** Touch the fingertips of the right *C hand* on the palm of the left *open hand* held in front of the chest, palm right and fingers pointing up, from the fingertips to the heel.

---- [sign continues] -->

dot pitch

- **space-between** Place the fingertips of the right *G hand*, palm down, between the index finger and middle finger of the left *5 hand*, palm in and fingers pointing right in front of the chest.

dots per inch See sign for DPI.

double-click[1] A method of pressing the mouse button twice in rapid succession to invoke a command.

- **double** Strike the middle finger of the right *V hand*, palm down, upward on the left *open hand*, palm up, by twisting the wrist, ending with the right palm facing up.

- **click** Beginning with the right index finger pointing forward in front of the chest, bend the finger deliberately downward.

double-click[2] (alternate sign)

- **two** Hold the right *2 hand*, palm back, in front of the right shoulder.

- **click** Beginning with the right index finger pointing forward in front of the chest, bend the finger deliberately downward.

double-density disk A disk capable of storing twice as much data as a single-density disk. Compare HIGH-DENSITY DISK.

- Fingerspell: D-D
- **disk** Move the fingertips of the right *D hand*, palm facing down and index finger pointing forward, in a double circle on the upturned left *open hand*.

down Describing a piece of computer equipment that has temporarily stopped working. Compare UP.

- **down** Jerk the extended thumb of the right *10 hand* downward, palm forward.

download 1. To copy a file from a main source to a peripheral device, such as loading a font from a computer to the printer. 2. To copy a file from a remote computer, such as a network file server, to a personal computer. Same sign used for **import**. Compare UPLOAD.

- **download** Beginning with both *V hands*, palms facing each other and fingers pointing up, near the right shoulder, bring the hands down to the left while bending the extended fingers.

downtime The length of time a computer system is inoperative due to a malfunction. Compare UPTIME.

- **down** Jerk the extended thumb of the right *10 hand* downward, palm forward.

- **time** Tap the bent index finger of the right *X hand*, palm down, with a double movement on the wrist of the downturned left hand.

dpi Acronym for *dots per inch*, which indicates the resolution of an image for a scanner or printer. The more dots per inch, the higher the resolution and quality of the image.

- Fingerspell: D-P-I

draft Referring to printing produced in less than letter-quality mode.

- **rough** Move the fingertips of the right *curved 5 hand*, palm down, from the heel to the fingertips of the left *open hand* held in front of the body, palm up.

drag

drag To hold down the mouse button while the mouse is moved, as to move a graphic, move a file from one directory to another, move a portion of text to a nearby place in a document, or to block text.

- **click** Beginning with the right index finger pointing forward in front of the chest, bend the finger deliberately downward.

- **drag** Move the right *X hand*, palm down, from in front of the right side of the chest downward to the left.

drag-and-drop The process of holding down the mouse button to move an object across the screen as a command, such as dragging a document onto a printer icon to print the document.

- **click** Beginning with the right index finger pointing forward in front of the chest, bend the finger deliberately downward.

- **drag** Move the right *X hand*, palm down, from in front of the right side of the chest downward to the left.

- **drop** Beginning with the right *X hand*, palm down in front of the body, flick the right index finger up.

draw program A graphics program that permits creation of graphical objects on the screen, such as lines, boxes, and circles.

- **draw** Move the fingertips of the right *D hand*, palm left, down the palm of the left *open hand* with a wavy movement.

---- [sign continues] ---→

■ **program** Move the middle finger of the right *P hand*, palm left, from the fingertips to the base of the left *open hand*, palm right and fingers pointing up. Repeat the movement on the back side of the left hand.

drive Short for *disk drive*. See sign for DISK DRIVE.

driver A program containing a series of instructions to the computer to reformat data for transfer to and from a peripheral device.

■ Fingerspell: D-R-I-V-E-R

drop-down menu See sign for MENU.

drum See sign for CYLINDER.

DSL Initialism for *digital subscriber line*, a type of high-speed, broadband, always-on connection to the Internet installed over standard telephone lines, usually able to operate without interfering with incoming or outgoing telephone calls.

■ Fingerspell: D-S-L

dumb terminal or **network computer** A display terminal with minimal input/output capabilities. Since it cannot process information alone, it interacts with a remote smart terminal. Compare SMART TERMINAL.

■ **dumb** Hit the palm side of the right *A hand* against the forehead.

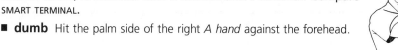

■ **terminal** Beginning with the index-finger sides of both *T hands* together in front of the chest, palms facing down, bring the hands apart to in front of each shoulder and then straight down.

dump 1. To transfer the entire contents of a file to a printer, display monitor, or storage without regard to format or readability. 2. Such a transfer. Related form: **dumping**.

■ **dump** Beginning with the fingers of the right *D hand,* palm facing down and index finger pointing forward, on the palm of the left *open hand,* palm facing up, bring the right hand downward to the right in an arc, ending with the palm facing up in front of the right side of the body.

duplicate

duplicate See sign for COPY.

dynamic Referring to computer circuitry that performs tasks as needed rather than in advance.

■ **dynamic** Beginning with both *D hands* in front of each side of the body, palms facing down and fingers pointing forward, move the hands straight forward simultaneously.

Dynamic Link Library See sign for DLL.

dynamic memory Computer memory that must constantly be refreshed. Compare STATIC MEMORY.

■ **dynamic** Beginning with both *D hands* in front of each side of the body, palms facing down and fingers pointing forward, move the hands straight forward simultaneously.

■ **memory** Beginning with the fingertips of the right *curved hand* touching the right side of the forehead, palm down, bring the hand forward and down while closing the fingers into an *S hand*, palm in.

EBCDIC Acronym for *Extended Binary Coded Decimal Interchange Code.* A standardized, proprietary 8-bit code used on large IBM computers to represent English characters as numbers, making it possible to transfer data from one IBM computer to another. Compare ASCII.

- Fingerspell: E-B-C-D-I-C

edit To make corrections or changes in a program or data.

- **edit** With the extended right index finger, palm forward, make small repeated crosses on the palm of the left *open hand,* palm in, in front of the chest.

editor or **text editor** A computer program designed to create and make changes to text files.

- **edit** With the extended right index finger, palm forward, make small repeated crosses on the palm of the left *open hand,* palm in, in front of the chest.

- **person marker** Move both *open hands,* palms facing each other, downward along the sides of the body.

electronic Pertaining to the flow of electricity through semi-conductors, valves, and filters, which is the essence of computer technology.

- **electric** Tap the knuckles of the index fingers of both *X hands* together, palms facing in, with a double movement.

electronic bulletin board See sign for ELECTRONIC MESSAGE CENTER.

electronic mail See signs for E-MAIL[1,2,3].

electronic message center or electronic bulletin board

A computer system that allows someone to post a message and maintains a list of messages that people can call up to read.

■ **electric** Tap the knuckles of the index fingers of both *X hands* together, palms facing in, with a double movement.

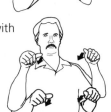

■ **bulletin board** Push the thumbs of both *10 hands,* forward with a short movement, palms facing forward, first in front of each shoulder and then in front of each side of the body.

■ **center** Move the right *open hand*, palm down, in a circular movement over the left *open hand,* palm up, bending the right fingers as the hand moves and ending with the fingertips of the right *bent hand* touching the middle of the left palm.

electronic stylus See sign for LIGHT PEN.

element An item of data within an array.

■ **elementary** Move the right *E hand,* palm forward, from side to s with a repeated movement below the left *open hand,* palm down and fingers pointing right, in front of the chest.

e-mail[1] or **mail** Short for *electronic mail.* Correspondence or data transmittedthrough a computer over telephone or cable lines or by means of a wireless connection.

■ **e-mail**[1] Hold the index-finger side of the left *B hand*, palm down and fingers pointing right, against the wrist of the right *E hand,* held in front of the right shoulder, palm forward.

■ **send** With a quick movement, flick the fingertips of the right *bent hand* forward across the back of the left *open hand*, both palms facing down, straightening the fingers as the right hand moves forward.

embedded command

e-mail² or **mail** (alternate sign)

- Fingerspell: E
- **letter** Touch the extended thumb of the right *10 hand* to the lips, palm in, and then move the thumb downward to touch the thumb of the left *10 hand* held in front of the chest, palm in.

e-mail³ or **mail** (alternate sign)

- **e-mail²** Move the extended right index finger from pointing left in front of the chest past the palm side of the left *C hand*, palm right, ending with the right index finger pointing forward.

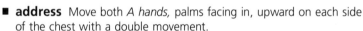

e-mail address A user-selected identification that, when coupled with the identification of the service provider or organization, becomes the location to and from which E-mail may be exchanged.

- Fingerspell: E
- **letter** Touch the extended thumb of the right *10 hand* to the lips, palm in, and then move the thumb downward to touch the thumb of the left *10 hand* held in front of the chest, palm in.

- **address** Move both *A hands,* palms facing in, upward on each side of the chest with a double movement.

embedded command In word processing, a sequence of special characters inserted in a document that affects the formatting of the document when it is printed.

- **penetrate** Move the fingers of the right *5 hand*, palm in and fingers pointing down, downward to mesh with the fingers of the left *5 hand* held in front of the chest, palm up and fingers pointing right.

- **order** Move the extended right index finger, palm left and finger pointing up, from in front of the mouth straight forward while turning the palm down, ending with the finger pointing forward.

enable

enable To switch a computer device on so it can operate. Compare DISABLE. Related form: **enabled**.

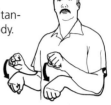

- **can** Move both *S hands,* palms facing down, downward simultaneously with a double movement in front of each side of the body.

encode To convert data into a code form that is acceptable to a specific piece of computer equipment. Compare DECODE.

- **encode** Beginning with the palms of both *E hands* together in front of the chest, twist the hands in opposite directions.

encoder A device that produces machine-readable output either from a manual keyboard or from data already recorded in some other code.

- **encode** Beginning with the palms of both *E hands* together in front of the chest, twist the hands in opposite directions.

- **person marker** Move both *open hands*, palms facing each other, downward along the sides of the body.

encryption The jumbling or coding of sensitive data to make it unreadable by another for security purposes. Same sign used for **garbage, garbled**.

- **mix** Beginning with the right *curved 5 hand* over the left *curved 5 hand*, palms facing each other, move the hands in repeated circles in front of the chest in opposite directions.

End key The keyboard key that moves the cursor to the end of a line, end of a page, or the end of the file, depending on the program that is running. In combination with another key, it may delete a portion of the document.

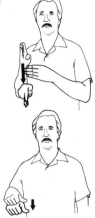

- **end** Beginning with the little-finger side of the right *B hand,* palm left, across the index-finger side of the left *B hand,* palm in, bring the right hand deliberately down off the left fingertips.

- **key** Push the extended thumb of the right *10 hand* downward a short distance in front of the right side of the body.

---

end user The person who uses a computer system or software after it has been fully developed.

- **end** Beginning with the little-finger side of the right *B hand,* palm left, across the index-finger side of the left *B hand,* palm in, bring the right hand deliberately down off the left fingertips.

- **use** Beginning with the heel of the right *U hand* on the back of the left *S hand,* move the right hand in a small upward circle.

- **person marker** Move both *open hands,* palms facing each other, downward along the sides of the body.

---

enter To add information into a computer, such as text to a document or records to a database. See sign for ACCESS.

Enter key or **Return key** The keyboard key that is pressed to execute a command or to move the cursor down to the next line.

- **return** Beginning with the right *R hand,* palm down and fingers pointing forward, in front of the right side of the chest, twist the hand over, ending with the palm facing up.

environment 1. Refers to the type of operating system, peripherals, and programs that make up a computer system. **2.** In DOS systems, an area in memory used to store various types of miscellaneous information, such as backup files.

- **environment** Move the right *E hand* in a circle around the extended left index finger, palm right and finger pointing up.

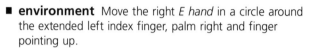

equipment See signs for DEVICE[1,2].

erase To remove data from computer storage without replacing it, such as a block of copy or a file. See sign for CLEAR[1].

error The general term used to refer to any deviation of a computed quantity from the correct or true value.

- **wrong** Bring the middle fingers of the right *Y hand*, palm in, back against the chin with a deliberate movement.

error message A note or message generated by an operating system or program and displayed on the monitor indicating that an error in processing has occurred and where it has occurred.

- **wrong** Bring the middle fingers of the right *Y hand*, palm in, back against the chin with a deliberate movement.

- **sentence** Beginning with the thumbs and index fingers of both *F hands* touching in front of the chest, palms facing each other, pull the hands apart with a double movement, ending in front of each side of the chest.

Esc Short for *Escape key.* A keyboard key that stops processing, returns the user to a previous stage of a process, or cancels a command.

- Fingerspell: E-S-C

escape[1], exit, or **quit** The command that quits a program and returns to a previous menu or operating level.

- **escape** Move the extended right index finger, palm left and finger pointing up, from between the index and middle fingers of the left *5 hand*, palm down in front of the chest, forward to the right with a deliberate movement.

escape², exit, or quit (alternate sign)

- **quit** Beginning with the extended fingers of the right *H hand* inside the opening of the left *O hand* held in front of the body, palm right, bring the right hand upward, ending in front of the right shoulder, palm left and fingers pointing up.

escape character A keyboard key that enters a nonprinting character when pressed, which signals the start of a printer or monitor control code.

- **escape** Move the extended right index finger, palm left and finger pointing up, from between the index and middle fingers of the left *5 hand*, palm down in front of the chest, forward to the right with a deliberate movement.

- **character** Move the right *C hand*, palm left, in a small circle and then back against the left side of the chest.

Escape key See sign for Esc.

escape sequence A set of special characters, usually beginning with an escape character, that sends a command to a device or program.

- **escape** Move the extended right index finger, palm left and finger pointing up, from between the index and middle fingers of the left *5 hand*, palm down in front of the chest, forward to the right with a deliberate movement.

- **process** Beginning with both *open hands* in front of the body, palms facing in, left fingers pointing right and right fingers pointing left, and the right hand closer to the chest than the left hand, move the left over the right hand and then the right over the left hand in an alternating movement.

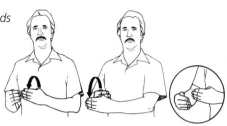

evaluation The process of determining if a newly designed computer system does what it was designed to do.

- **evaluate** Move both *E hands*, palms facing forward, up and down with a repeated alternating movement in front of each side of the chest.

event A keystroke or click of a mouse button that causes a procedure to respond.

- **happen** Beginning with both extended index fingers in front of the body, palms facing up and fingers pointing forward, flip the hands over toward each other, ending with the palms facing down.

event-driven programming A style of writing programs that waits for the user to press a key or mouse button, called an *event*, before doing anything else. Compare OBJECT-ORIENTED PROGRAMMING.

- **happen** Beginning with both extended index fingers in front of the body, palms facing up and fingers pointing forward, flip the hands over toward each other, ending with the palms facing down.

- **connect** Beginning with both *curved 5 hands* in front of each side of the body, palms facing each other, bring the hands together while touching the thumb and index fingertips of each hand and intersecting with each other.

- **program** Move the middle finger of the right *P hand*, palm left, from the fingertips to the base of the left *open hand*, palm right and fingers pointing up. Repeat the movement on the back side of the left hand.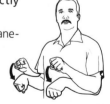

EXE An abbreviation for *executable*. A file extension identifying a program that can be directly executed.

- Fingerspell: E-X-E

executable See sign for EXE.

executable file A file in a format that the computer can directly execute. Compare SOURCE FILE.

- **can** Move both *S hands,* palms facing down, downward simultaneously with a double movement in front of each side of the body.

- **run** Brush the palm of the right *open hand* upward with a double movement across the left *open hand,* palms facing each other and fingers pointing forward.

execute or **run** To start a program or perform a task. Same sign used for **up**.

- **run** Brush the fingers of the right *open hand* across the palm of the left *open hand* held in front of the chest, palm facing right and fingers pointing forward.

exit See signs for ESCAPE[1,2].

expand or **explode** To decompress previously compressed files so that the computer can use them. Compare COMPRESS.

- **expand** Beginning with the little-finger side of the right *S hand* on top of the index-finger side of the left *S hand,* palms facing in opposite directions, bring the hands apart while opening into *curved 5 hands* in front of each side of the chest, palms facing each other.

expansion board[1]**, circuit board,** or **expansion card** A thin rectangular board containing or imprinted with various electronic components and microchips that can be inserted into a computer to provide additional capabilities, such as increased memory or graphics capabilities.

- **expand** Beginning with the little-finger side of the right *S hand* on top of the index-finger side of the left *S hand,* palms facing in opposite directions, bring the hands apart while opening into *curved 5 hands* in front of each side of the chest, palms facing each other.

- **board**[1] Bring the little-finger side of the right *B hand,* palm left, sharply against the palm of the left *C hand* held in front of the chest, palm up.

expansion board[2]**, circuit board,** or **expansion card** (alternate sign)

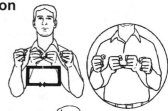

- **circuit** Beginning with the little fingers of both *I hands* touching in front of the chest, palms facing each other, bring the hands apart to in front of each side of the chest, straight down, and then together again to touch in front of the chest.

- **board**[2] Slide the little-finger side of the right *B hand,* palm left, between the thumb and index finger of the left *C hand* held in front of the chest, palm up.

expansion board

expansion board[3], circuit board, or expansion card
(alternate sign)

- **board[1]** Bring the little-finger side of the right *B hand*, palm left, sharply against the palm of the left *C hand* held in front of the chest, palm up.

expansion board[4], circuit board, or expansion card
(alternate sign)

- **add-to** Swing the right *5 hand* upward from the right side of the body while changing into a *flattened O hand,* ending with the right index finger touching the little-finger side of the left *flattened O hand* in front of the chest, both palms facing in.

- **card** Beginning with the fingertips of both *L hands* touching in front of the chest, palms forward, bring the hands apart to in front of each shoulder, and then pinch each thumb and index finger together.

expansion card See signs for EXPANSION BOARD[1,2,3,4].

expansion slot The physical opening in a computer into which the expansion card plugs.

- **expand** Beginning with the little-finger side of the right *S hand* on top of the index-finger side of the left *S hand,* palms facing in opposite directions, bring the hands apart while opening into *curved 5 hands* in front of each side of the chest, palms facing each other.

- Fingerspell: S-L-O-T

explode See sign for EXPAND.

export See sign for UPLOAD.

expression Used in programming to describe any legal combination of symbols or a formula that represents a value.

- **gather** Beginning with both *curved 5 hands* in front of each side of the chest, palms facing each other, bring the fingers together in front of the body.

---- [sign continues] --->

- **show** With the extended right index finger touching the palm of the left *open hand*, palm right, move both hands forward a short distance.

Extended Binary Coded Decimal Interchange Code See sign for EBCDIC.

Extensible Markup Language See sign for XML.

extension or **file extension** An optional suffix added to a filename, as in DOS or Windows, consisting of a dot (period) and up to three other characters, which helps to identify the type of file and the program that created it.

- Fingerspell: E-X-T

external Used to describe a drive, modem, or other peripheral that has its own case, cables, and power supply and plugs into a port of a computer. Compare INTERNAL.

- **outside** Beginning with the right *flattened O hand* inserted in the palm side of the left *C hand*, bring the right hand upward.

facsimile machine See sign for FAX MACHINE.

fail (of a computer, a computer system, or a software program) To stop working. Related form: **failure**.

- **fail** Beginning with the back of the right *V hand* on the heel of the left *open hand,* palm up, move the right hand across the left palm and off the fingers.

fatal error An error, as in user input or because of a software bug, that causes a program to abort prior to completion. See sign for CLOSE.

favorite See sign for BOOKMARK.

fax **1.** To send a document via a fax machine. **2.** A document that is sent via a fax machine. **3.** Short for a facsimile machine.

- Fingerspell: F-A-X

fax machine Short for *facsimile machine.* A machine used to send a printed page or image through phone lines to another machine that prints a copy.

- Fingerspell: F-A-X

- **machine** With the fingers of both *curved 5 hands* loosely meshed together, palms facing in, move the hands up and down in front of the chest with a repeated movement.

feed **1.** To manually insert paper into a printer. **2.** The mechanical process whereby lengthy materials move along the required operating positions.

- **feed** Push both *flattened O hands*, palms facing up and fingers pointing forward, one hand somewhat forward of the other hand, forward with a short double movement.

feedback[1] A process wherein output or information from a sequential task serves to modify subsequent tasks.

- **feedback**[1] Beginning with the right *F hand* in front of the right side of the body, palm left, move the hand back toward the right shoulder while changing into a *B hand*, palm facing in.

feedback[2] *n.* (alternate sign)

- **feedback**[2] Beginning with both *F hands* in front of each side of the chest, right palm forward and left palm in, move the hands with a double movement in opposite directions to and from the chest.

female connector A type of plug that consists of holes into which a corresponding male connector plugs. Compare MALE CONNECTOR.

- **female** Beginning with the thumb of the right *A hand* on the chin, bring the hand downward while opening into a *5 hand*, ending with the thumb touching the chest.

- **plug** Move the right *V hand*, palm down, forward from in front of the right shoulder, ending with the fingers of the right *V hand* on either side of the extended left index finger held pointing up in front of the chest, palm right.

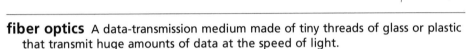

fiber optics A data-transmission medium made of tiny threads of glass or plastic that transmit huge amounts of data at the speed of light.

- Fingerspell: F-O

field Space reserved for a single piece of information in a database program. A record is made up of one or more fields. See sign for COLUMN.

file A set of related information as identified by a filename and stored as a unit. There are many types of files that store different types of information, such as *data files, program files, text files,* etc.

- **file** Slide the little-finger side of the right *B hand*, palm angled up, between the fingers of the left *5 hand*, palm facing in, first with between the index and middle fingers and then between the middle and ring fingers.

file extension See sign for EXTENSION.

file folder or **folder** A special kind of file used to organize other files, facilitating their retrieval.

- **file** Slide the little-finger side of the right *B hand*, palm angled up, between the fingers of the left *5 hand*, palm facing in, first with between the index and middle fingers and then between the middle and ring fingers.

---- [sign continues] -->

file folder

■ **book** Beginning with the palms of both *open hands* together in front of the chest, fingers angled forward, bring the hands apart at the top while keeping the little fingers together.

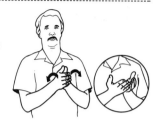

file manager A software utility that simplifies the task of locating and organizing files.

■ **file** Slide the little-finger side of the right *B hand*, palm angled up, between the fingers of the left *5 hand*, palm facing in, first between the index and middle fingers and then between the middle and ring fingers.

■ **plan** Move both *open hands* from in front of the left side of the body, palms facing each other and fingers pointing forward, in a long smooth movement to in front of the right side of the body.

filename The designation that identifies a specific file.

■ **file** Slide the little-finger side of the right *B hand*, palm angled up, between the fingers of the left *5 hand*, palm facing in, first between the index and middle fingers and then between the middle and ring fingers.

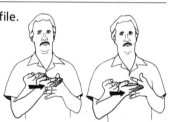

■ **name** Tap the middle-finger side of the right *H hand* across the index-finger side of the left *H hand* with a double movement.

file server See sign for NETWORK SERVER.

fill In computer graphics, a function that allows the inside of a defined area to be filled with shading, a color, or a texture.

■ **inside** Insert the fingertips of the right *flattened O hand*, palm down, into the center of the thumb side of the left *O hand*, palm right, with a short double movement.

---- [sign continues] --->

- **color** Wiggle the fingers of the right *5 hand* in front of the mouth, fingers pointing up and palm facing in.

filter **1.** A program that accepts a certain type of data as input, transforms it, and then outputs the transformed data. **2.** A machine-controlled pattern through which data is passed, permitting only data that matches the pattern to pass through.

- **filter** Beginning with fingers of the left *4 hand* across the back of the fingers of the right *4 hand*, both palms facing in, bring the hands downward and apart with a double movement.

find The ability of the computer to search within a document for a specific series of characters. Compare SEARCH.

- **find** Beginning with right *5 hand* in front of the right side of the body, palm down, bring the hand upward while closing the thumb and index finger, forming an *F hand*.

find and replace, global search and replace, or **search and replace** A command to look for specific characters in a file so as to substitute other specific characters.

- **search** Move the right *C hand*, palm left, with a double circular movement in front of the face.

- **and** Move the right *5 hand*, palm in and fingers pointing left, from in front of the left side of the body to the right while closing the fingers to a *flattened O hand*.

- **exchange** Beginning with both *modified X hands* in front of the body, right hand somewhat forward of the left hand, move the right hand back toward the body in an upward arc while moving the left hand forward with a downward arc.

firewall

firewall A protective hardware or software barrier that prevents others, especially through the Internet, from gaining unauthorized access to sensitive information on a computer or private network.

- **fire** Move both *5 hands*, palms facing up, from in front of the waist upward in front of the chest while wiggling the fingers.

- **wall** Beginning with the index-finger sides of both *B hands* together in front of the chest, palms facing forward and fingers pointing up, bring the hands apart to in front of each shoulder.

FireWire A fast data-transfer cable onto which up to 63 devices can be connected to a Macintosh computer by daisy-chaining them together.

- **cable** Beginning with the index-finger side of both *C hands* touching in front of the body, palms facing down, bring the right hand outward to the right.
- Fingerspell: F-I-R-E-W-I-R-E

fixed 1. Referring to a field that always exists within a data record. 2. Referring to the preset length of a field or data record that does not vary within the database.

- **lock** Beginning with the little-finger side of the right *S hand* above the left *S hand*, both palms down, turn the right hand over, ending with the back of the right hand, palm up, on the back of the left hand, palm down.

fixed disk See sign for HARD DISK.

fixed spacing The printing of characters at fixed horizontal intervals on a page.

- **lock** Beginning with the little-finger side of the right *S hand* above the left *S hand*, both palms down, turn the right hand over, ending with the back of the right hand, palm up, on the back of the left hand, palm down.

- **leading** Place the fingertips of the right *G hand*, palm down, between the index finger and middle finger of the left *5 hand*, palm in and fingers pointing right in front of the chest.

flag An indicator used to mark a particular condition or status. The flag is said to be *set* when it is turned on.

- **flag** With the extended left index finger touching the right wrist, wave the right *open hand* back and forth with a repeated movement in front of the right shoulder.

---

flatbed scanner A type of optical scanner that has a flat surface on which to lay documents to be scanned.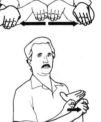

- **floor** Beginning with the index-finger side of both *B hands* touching in front of the waist, palms facing down and fingers pointing forward, move the hands apart to each side.

- **scan** Move the bent index finger of the right *X hand,* palm left, back and forth with a repeated movement under the palm of the left *open hand,* palm down.

---

flat-panel screen See sign for DISPLAY SCREEN.

---

flip-flop See sign for TOGGLE.

---

float or **slack time** The amount of time following the completion of a task and the start of the next task.

- **float** Beginning with the right *F hand* in front of the right side of the chest, palm forward, move the hand with a wavy movement to the right.

---

floppy disk See signs for DISK[1,2].

---

flow The sequence of events in a computer program.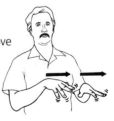

- **flow** Beginning with both *open hands* in front of each side of the chest, palms facing down and fingers pointing forward, move the hands forward while wiggling the fingers.

---

flowchart A diagram consisting of lines and symbols that represent the logic and sequence of a program.

- Fingerspell: F-C

folder

folder See sign for FILE FOLDER.

font A design for a collection of type characters consisting of a combination of typeface, size, pitch, and spacing.
- Fingerspell: F-O-N-T

forced page break See sign for HARD PAGE BREAK.

foreground The activity, in a multitasking operating system, that is in view and under the control of the user. Compare BACKGROUND.
- **foreground** In quick succession tap the index-finger side of the right *F hand* and then *G hand,* palm facing forward, against the left *open hand,* palm facing right and fingers pointing up.

form A user-friendly means of viewing the data stored in a record that makes the database easier to use. Same sign used for format[4].
- **form** Beginning with the fingertips of both *F hands* touching in front of the chest, palms facing each other, bring the hands away from each other to about shoulder width and then straight down a short distance, ending with the palms facing forward.

format[1] or **initialize** To prepare a floppy or hard disk for storing programs or data. Related form: **formatted**.
- **erase** Rub the little-finger side of the right *S hand,* palm in, back and forth with a repeated movement on the palm of the left *open hand,* palm up.

- **disk** Move the fingertips of the right *D hand,* palm down and index finger pointing forward, in a double circle on the upturned left *open hand.*

format[2] or **initialize** (alternate sign) Related form: **formatted**.
- **format**[1] Beginning with the right *F hand* in front of the right side of the chest, palm forward, and the left *open hand* in front of the left side of the chest, palm right, move the right hand forward in a circular movement and then against the palm of the left *open hand.*

format[3] or **initialize** (alternate sign) Related form: **formatted**.

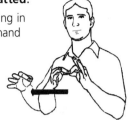

- **format**[2] Beginning with the fingers of both *F hands* touching in front of the chest, palms facing each other, bring the right hand outward to the right.

format[4] In word processing, spreadsheets, etc., the layout or arrangement of information in a document and the choice of fonts with which to display it. See sign for FORM.

formula A rule expressed as an equation.

- **formula** Beginning with the index-finger side of the right *F hand,* palm forward, against the fingers of the left *open hand,* palm right, move the right hand downward to touch the left hand near the heel.

formula translater See sign for FORTRAN.

FORTRAN Acronym for *Formula Translator*. A programming language that permits programmers to write mathematical formulas normally and that runs on different types of computers with little modification.

- Fingerspell: F-O-R-T-R-A-N

forum See sign for NEWSGROUP.

forward slash or **slash** 1. A symbol (/) used in text to separate related items as in back/forth, up/down, or his/hers. 2. In computer math, the symbol used for division, e.g., 12/4 means "twelve divided by four." 3. A character (/) used to separate directory and file names in some operating systems, such as UNIX. 4. A keyboard key that inserts this character or symbol.

- **slash** Bring the right *B hand*, palm left, from in front of the right shoulder downward to the left with a deliberate movement.

4GL See sign for FOURTH-GENERATION LANGUAGE

fourth-generation language or **4GL** Any of the high-level programming languages that are close to human language in their construction.

- Fingerspell: 4-G-L

freeware See signs for SHAREWARE[1,2].

front end A program, portion of a program, or computer that hides the details, such as the user interface.

- **front** Move the right *open hand*, palm facing in and fingers pointing left, straight down from in front of the face to in front of the chest.

- **end** Move the palm side of the right *open hand*, palm left and fingers pointing forward, deliberately down past the fingertips of the left *open hand*, palm in and fingers pointing right.

---

front panel See sign for CONSOLE.

---

frozen (of a computer system or program) Unable to respond to input from the keyboard or mouse. See signs for HANG-UP[1,2].

full backup[1] or **system backup** 1. Making a safety or reserved copy of every program and data file on the computer system. 2. The safety or reserved copy that is made.

- **full** Slide the palm of the right *open hand*, palm down, from right to left across the index-finger side of the left *S hand*, palm right.

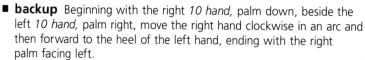

- **backup** Beginning with the right *10 hand*, palm down, beside the left *10 hand*, palm right, move the right hand clockwise in an arc and then forward to the heel of the left hand, ending with the right palm facing left.

---

full backup[2] or **system backup** (alternate sign)

- **system** Beginning with the index-finger sides of both *5 hands* touching in front of the chest, palms down, move the hands outward to in front of each shoulder and then straight down a short distance.

- **backup** Beginning with the right *10 hand*, palm down, beside the left *10 hand*, palm right, move the right hand clockwise in an arc and then forward to the heel of the left hand, ending with the right palm facing left.

---

function A subprogram, or a smaller part of the main program that performs a specific task. Related form: **functional.**

- **function** Move the fingertips of the right *F hand,* palm forward, back and forth across the length of the index-finger side of the left *B hand,* palm down, with a double movement.

---

fuzzy logic A method of handling imprecision by using a range of values, useful, for example, in artificial intelligence programs and spellcheckers.

- Fingerspell: F-U-Z-Z-Y
- **logic** Move the right *L hand,* palm forward, in a double circle in front of the right side of the forehead.

game Something played on a computer through interactive software that falls into one of three types: arcade, strategy, and board.

- **game** Bring the knuckles of both *10 hands,* palms in, against each other with a double movement in front of the chest.

---

garbage Unwanted or meaningless data carried in a computer's storage. See sign for ENCRYPTION.

---

garbled See sign for ENCRYPTION.

GB See sign for GIGABYTE.

---

generality or **general purpose** The solution of a problem in a computer program that is done in such a way that it serves a variety of other users with the same general kind of problem.

- **general** Beginning with both *open hands* in front of the chest, fingers angled toward each other, swing the fingers away from each other, ending with the fingers angled outward in front of each side of the body.

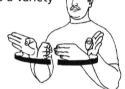

---

general purpose See sign for GENERALITY.

---

generate To process or create, as to generate a report from computer data, to generate an index from marked terms in a document, or to generate a new program.

- **generate** Beginning with the little-finger side of the right *G hand* on the index-finger side of the left *G hand,* palms facing in opposite directions, twist the hands in opposite directions by bending the wrists.

---

generator A computer program designed to create other programs or routines for other programs.

- **generate** Beginning with the little-finger side of the right *G hand* on the index-finger side of the left *G hand,* palms facing in opposite directions, twist the hands in opposite directions by bending the wrists.

---- [sign continues] -->

■ **person marker** Move both *open hands*, palms facing each other, downward along the sides of the body.

Ghz See sign for GIGAHERTZ.

GIF (pronounced *jif*) An acronym for *Graphics Interchange Format*. A bit-mapped file format used to store graphics.

■ Fingerspell: G-I-F

---

gigabyte or **GB** About one thousand million (one billion) bytes.

■ Fingerspell: G-B

---

gigahertz or **Ghz** The speed of microprocessors, the clock speed, measured in gigahertz, which is approximately one billion cycles per second. Compare MEGA-HERTZ.

■ Fingerspell: G-H-Z

---

glitch A problem that causes a program or computer system not to work properly.

■ **problem** Beginning with the knuckles of both *bent V hands*, touching in front of the chest, twist the hands in opposite directions with a deliberate movement, rubbing the knuckles against each other.

---

global Referring to formatting or instructions that act on all like elements in a computer file.

■ **global** Beginning with both *G hands* in front of the body, right hand above the left, palms facing in opposite directions, roll the hands over each other in a forward circle, ending with the little-finger side of the right *G hand* on the index-finger side of the left *G hand*.

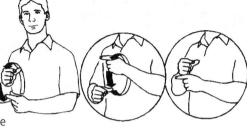

---

global search and replace See sign for FIND AND REPLACE.

Gopher A predecessor to the World Wide Web used for searching the Internet.

■ Fingerspell: G-O-P-H-E-R

graph

graph or **chart** A visual representation of numeric quantities showing their relationship. Same sign used for: **schedule**.

- **graph** Beginning with the left *open hand* held in front of the left shoulder, palm right and fingers pointing forward, bring the fingers of the right *4 hand*, palm left, down the heel of the left hand, and then drag the back of the right fingers across the length of the left palm from the heel to the fingertips.

graphical user interface or **GUI** (pronounced *goo-ee*) A program that takes advantage of the computer's graphics capabilities to make other programs easy to use through use of a mouse or other pointing device, icons, and pull-down menus.

- Fingerspell: G-U-I

graphics The process used to display computer data pictorially.

- **graphics** Move the little-finger side of the right *G hand*, palm in, with a wiggly movement across the palm of the left *open hand* held in front of the chest.

graphics accelerator Hardware or a software program designed to improve a computer's graphics performance.

- **graphics** Move the little-finger side of the right *G hand*, palm in, with a wiggly movement across the palm of the left *open hand* held in front of the chest.

- **fast** Beginning with the extended index fingers of both *one hands* pointing forward in front of the chest, pull the hands back toward the chest while changing to *S hands*.

- **person marker** Move both *open hands*, palms facing each other, downward along the sides of the body.

graphics adapter board See signs for GRAPHICS ADAPTER CARD[1,2].

---

graphics adapter card[1], graphics adapter board, video card, or video adapter
A graphics card, which plugs into an expansion slot, that provides the means for displaying graphics on a monitor screen.

- **graphics** Move the little-finger side of the right *G hand*, palm in, with a wiggly movement across the palm of the left *open hand* held in front of the chest.

- **change**[1] With the palm side of both *S hands* facing each other, twist the wrists in opposite directions in order to reverse positions.

- **card** Beginning with the fingertips of both *L hands* touching in front of the chest, palms facing forward, bring the hands apart to in front of each shoulder, and then pinch each thumb and index finger together.

---

graphics adapter card[2], graphics adapter board, video card, or video adapter (alternate sign)

- **video** With the thumb of the right *5 hand*, palm forward, against the palm of the left *open hand,* palm left and fingers pointing up, wiggle the right fingers.

- **card** Beginning with the fingertips of both *L hands* touching in front of the chest, palms facing forward, bring the hands apart to in front of each shoulder, and then pinch each thumb and index finger together.

---

graphics file The type of document file created by a graphics application.

- **graphics** Move the little-finger side of the right *G hand*, palm in, with a wiggly movement across the palm of the left *open hand* held in front of the chest.

---- [sign continues] -->

graphics File

- **file** Slide the little-finger side of the right *B hand,* palm angled up, between the fingers of the left *5 hand,* palm facing in, first between the index and middle fingers and then between the middle and ring fingers.

Graphics Interchange Format See sign for GIF.

graphics program See sign for GRAPHICS SOFTWARE.

graphics software or **graphics program** Any of the programs that let the computer produce graphics.

- **graphics** Move the little-finger side of the right *G hand,* palm in, with a wiggly movement across the palm of the left *open hand* held in front of the chest.

- **program** Move the middle finger of the right *P hand,* palm left, from the fingertips to the base of the left *open hand,* palm right and fingers pointing up. Repeat the movement on the back side of the left hand.

groupware Software designed for sharing information and communicating easily among networked PCs.

- **group** Beginning with both *C hands* in front of the right side of the chest, palms facing each other, bring the hands away from each other in outward arcs while turning the palms in, ending with the little fingers near each other.

- **interact** With the thumb of the left *A hand* pointing up and the thumb of the right *A hand* pointing down, circle the thumbs around each other while moving the hands from left to right in front of the chest.

GUI See sign for GRAPHICAL USER INTERFACE.

---

hacker Someone who is knowledgeable and enthusiastic about computers and programming and pushes computer systems to the highest level of performance. Compare CRACKER.

- Fingerspell: H-A-C-K-E-R

---

halftone A black-and-white copy of a photograph in which dark shades are represented by thick dots and light shades are represented by filling the area less densely with smaller dots.

- **picture** Move the right *C hand*, palm forward, from near the right side of the face downward, ending with the index-finger side of the right *C hand* against the palm of the left *open hand* held in front of the chest, palm right.

- **black** Pull the side of the extended right index finger, palm down and finger pointing left, from left to right across the forehead.

- **white** Beginning with the fingertips of the right *curved 5 hand* on the chest, pull the hand forward while closing the fingers into a *flattened O hand*.

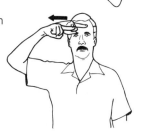

- **grey** Beginning with both *5 hands* in front of the chest, fingers pointing toward each other and palms facing in, move the hands forward and back in opposite directions, lightly brushing fingertips as the hands pass each other.

---

handheld computer See sign for PALMTOP COMPUTER.

handshake

handshake The process by which two devices establish communication.

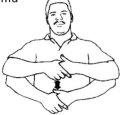

- **handshake** Grasp the left *open hand* with the right *curved hand,* both palms facing in, and shake the hands up and down with a double movement.

hands-on A teaching process that allows the learner to learn by physically using the computer.

- **hands** Beginning with the little-finger side of the right *open hand* at an angle on the thumb side of the left *open hand,* palms angled in, bring the right hand up the back of the left hand. Exchange positions and repeat the movement with the left hand.

- **on** Bring the palm of the right *open hand* downward on the back of the left *open hand* held in front of the body, both palms facing down.

hang-up[1] An unwanted halt in a computer's functioning so that it does not respond to input from the keyboard or mouse. Same sign used for **frozen.**

- **hang** With the index finger of the right *X hand,* palm left, over the left extended index finger, palm down, move both hands downward a short distance.

hang-up[2] (alternate sign)

- **not** Bring the extended thumb of the right *10 hand* from under the chin, palm left, forward with a deliberate movement.

- **respond** Beginning with the fingers of both *R hands* pointing up, right hand closer to the mouth than the left hand and the palms facing each other, move the hands forward and downward with a deliberate movement, ending with the palms facing down and fingers pointing forward.

hard copy A printed copy of all or part of a computer file.

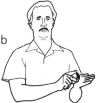

- **print** Beginning with the thumb of the right *G hand* on the heel of the left *open hand*, tap the right index finger down to the thumb with a double movement.

- **copy**[1] Move the fingers of the right *curved hand* from touching the palm of the left *open hand* while closing the right fingers and thumb forming a *flattened O hand*.

---

hard disk or **fixed disk** A disk that is mounted with its own drive, usually installed in the computer case.

- **hard** Strike the little-finger side of the right *bent V hand* sharply against the index-finger side of the left *bent V hand*, palms facing in opposite directions.

- **disk** Move the fingertips of the right *D hand*, palm facing down and index finger pointing forward, in a double circle on the upturned left *open hand*.

---

hard drive[1] or **HD** The device that contains the hard disk.

- **hard** Strike the little-finger side of the right *bent V hand* sharply against the index-finger side of the left *bent V hand*, palms facing in opposite directions.
- Fingerspell: D-R-I-V-E

---

hard drive[2] or **HD** (alternate sign)

- Fingerspell: H-D

---

hard page break or **forced page break** The command causing a word processor to end a page and start a new page regardless of whether the preceding page is full to the set margins. Compare SOFT PAGE BREAK.

- **hard** Strike the little-finger side of the right *bent V hand* sharply against the index-finger side of the left *bent V hand*, palms facing in opposite directions.

---- [sign continues] --->

hard page break

- **page** Strike the extended thumb of the right *10 hand*, palm down, against the left open palm with a double circular movement.

- **break** Beginning with both *S hands* in front of the body, index fingers touching and palms down, move the hands away from each other while twisting the wrists with a deliberate movement, ending with the palms facing each other.

hard return The command causing a word processor to jump from the end of one line of text to the beginning of the next line regardless of whether the preceding line is full to the set margin. Compare SOFT RETURN.

- **hard** Strike the little-finger side of the right *bent V hand* sharply against the index-finger side of the left *bent V hand*, palms facing in opposite directions.

- **return** Beginning with the right *R hand*, palm down and fingers pointing forward, in front of the right side of the chest, twist the hand over, ending with the palm facing up.

hardware[1] The physical parts of a computer, such as the cpu, printer, modem, monitor, and keyboard; the parts that you can touch. Compare SOFTWARE.

- Fingerspell: H-W

hardware[2] See signs for DEVICE[1,2].

hash coding See sign for HASH VALUES.

hashing See sign for HASH VALUES.

hash values, hash coding, or **hashing** A key-to-address transformation in which the keys determine the location of the data.

- Fingerspell: H-A-S-H

- **value** Beginning with the index fingers of both *V hands* touching in front of the chest, palms facing down, move the hands outward and upward in arcs, ending with the index fingers touching and the palms facing forward.

HD See signs for HARD DRIVE[1,2].

head The part in a disk drive that reads data from or writes data to a disk or tape.

- **head** Touch the fingertips of the right *bent hand,* palm down, first to the right side of the forehead and then to the right side of the chin.

help A program feature that provides guidance to the user, such as explaining commands or giving instructions for performing various tasks.

- **help** With the little-finger side of the right *A hand* in the upturned left *open hand,* move both hands upward in front of the chest.

hex See sign for HEXADECIMAL.

hexadecimal, base sixteen, or **hex** A numbering system using base 16 as opposed to base 10 (decimal), which consists of 16 unique symbols: the numbers *0* to *9* and the letters *A* to *F.*

- **hexadecimal** Beginning with the right *B hand,* palm forward and fingers pointing up, under the palm of the left *open hand,* palm down and fingers pointing right, move the right hand to the right while forming the number *16.*

hidden files Files that don't appear in a normal directory listing, hidden so as to prevent viruses or accidental erasing or altering.

- **hide** Move the thumb of the right *A hand,* palm facing left, from near the mouth downward in an arc to under the left *curved hand* held in front of the chest, palm down.

- **file** Slide the little-finger side of the right *B hand,* palm angled up, between the fingers of the left *5 hand,* palm facing in, first between the index and middle fingers and then between the middle and ring fingers.

hierarchical Referring to systems that are organized in the shape of an inverted tree, in which the top-most item has branches that in turn branch to other items, with further branching as necessary. Related form: **hierarchy.**

- **hierarchical** Beginning with the fingertips of both *H hands* touching in front of the chest, palms facing in, bring the hands apart to in front of each shoulder. Then move the *H hands* downward, palms facing each other and fingers pointing forward, outward to in front of each side of the chest, and downward again.

hierarchy chart

hierarchy chart See sign for STRUCTURE CHART.

---

high-capacity disk See signs for HIGH-DENSITY DISK[1,2].

---

high-density disk or **high-capacity disk** A disk capable of storing more data than a double-density disk, such as the common 3½-inch floppy disk, which has a capacity of 1.44 megabytes. Compare DOUBLE-DENSITY DISK.

- Fingerspell: H-D
- **disk** Move the fingertips of the right *D hand,* palm facing down and index finger pointing forward, in a double circle on the upturned left *open hand.*

---

high-density disk or **high-capacity disk** (alternate sign)

- **high** Move the right *H hand,* palm in, upward in front of the chest.

- **density** Shake the right *D hand,* palm forward, in front of the chest.

- **disk** Move the fingertips of the right *D hand,* palm facing down and index finger pointing forward, in a double circle on the upturned left *open hand.*

---

high-level language or **high-order language** A programming language containing commands that nearly resemble English, such as BASIC and Pascal, instead of a machine code. Compare LOW-LEVEL LANGUAGE.

- **high** Move the right *H hand,* palm in, upward in front of the chest.

- **plan** Move both *open hands* from in front of the left side of the body, palms facing each other and fingers pointing forward, in a long smooth movement to in front of the right side of the body.

---- [sign continues] -->

- **language** Beginning with the thumbs of both *L hands* near each other in front of the chest, palms angled down, bring the hands outward with a wavy movement to in front of each side of the chest.

---

highlight See sign for BLOCK.

---

high-order language See sign for HIGH-LEVEL LANGUAGE.

---

high resolution Pertaining to a high number of pixels in an image that enable the picture to exhibit fine detail and high quality.

- **clear** Beginning with the fingertips of both *flattened O hands* touching in front of the chest, palms facing each other, move the hands quickly upward in arcs to above each shoulder while opening to *5 hands*.

- **quality** Shake the right *Q hand*, palm down and fingers pointing down, in front of the chest.

---

high-speed access The ability of a program or device to locate a single piece of information and make it available to the computer for processing as measured in nanoseconds.

- **high** Move the right *H hand*, palm in, upward in front of the chest.

- **fast** Beginning with the extended index fingers of both *one hands* pointing forward in front of the chest, pull the hands back toward the chest while changing to *S hands*.

- **enter** Move the back of the right *open hand* forward in a downward arc under the palm of the left *open hand*, both palms down.

high-tech *Informal.* Referring to the latest, most-sophisticated devices available to the consumer.

- **high** Move the right *H hand*, palm in, upward in front of the chest.

- **technology** Tap the bent middle finger of the right *5 hand*, palm up, upward on the little-finger side of the left *open hand*, palm right and fingers pointing forward, with a double movement.

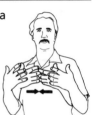

---

hit or **match** An accurate match in a database search, such as of a character string.

- **match** Beginning with both *5 hands* in front of each side of the chest, palms facing in, bring the hands together, ending with the bent fingers of both hands meshed together in front of the chest.

---

hold down A command, as in some word-processing programs, to hold down two or more keys on the keyboard simultaneously.

- **press-down** With a deliberate movement, push the extended thumb of the right *10 hand* downward a short distance in front of the right side of the body, holding the final position.

---

home The starting position for the cursor on a display screen.

- **home** Touch the fingertips of the right *flattened O hand* first to the right side of the chin, palm down and then to the right cheek.

Home key A keyboard key that controls cursor movement, sending it to any of several positions in a file depending on which program is running.

- **home** Touch the fingertips of the right *flattened O hand* first to the right side of the chin, palm down, and then to the right cheek.

---- [sign continues] -->

- **key** Push the extended thumb of the right *10 hand* downward a short distance in front of the right side of the body.

home page The initial page that appears on the World Wide Web when the browser is started.

- **home** Touch the fingertips of the right *flattened O hand* first to the right side of the chin, palm down, and then to the right cheek.

- **page** Strike the extended thumb of the right *10 hand*, palm down, against the left open palm with a double circular movement.

host computer A computer system that is accessed through a modem by a user working at a remote location.

- Fingerspell: H-O-S-T
- **computer**[1] Move the thumb side of the right *C hand,* palm left, from touching the lower part of the extended left arm upward to touch the upper arm.

host processor See sign for MAINFRAME COMPUTER.

hot key A user-defined key that executes a command that otherwise would require several key strokes. Compare MACRO.

- **hot** Beginning with the right *curved 5 hand* in front of the mouth, palm in, twist the wrist forward with a deliberate movement while moving the hand downward a short distance.

- **key** Push the extended thumb of the right *10 hand* downward a short distance in front of the right side of the body.

hot link

hot link A link between two applications such that changes in one cause corresponding changes to be made in the other.

- **hot** Beginning with the right *curved 5 hand* in front of the mouth, palm in, twist the wrist forward with a deliberate movement while moving the hand downward a short distance.

- **connect** Beginning with both *curved 5 hands* in front of each side of the body, palms facing each other, bring the hands together while touching the thumb and index fingertips of each hand and intersecting with each other.

---

hot plugging See sign for HOT SWAPPING.

---

hot swapping or **hot plugging** The ability of a computer and its operating system to accept a peripheral's being plugged into or removed from a port, such as a USB port or a PCMCIA expansion slot, without requiring that the computer be turned off first.

- **hot** Beginning with the right *curved 5 hand* in front of the mouth, palm in, twist the wrist forward with a deliberate movement while moving the hand downward a short distance.

- **exchange** Beginning with both *modified X hands* in front of the body, right hand somewhat forward of the left hand, move the right hand back toward the body in an upward arc while moving the left hand forward with a downward arc.

---

housekeeping The process of organizing, deleting, and backing up files and putting them in their proper directories in order to maintain an orderly file structure for efficient operation.

- **house** Beginning with the fingertips of both *open hands* touching in front of the neck, palms angled toward each other, bring the hands at a downward angle outward to in front of each shoulder.

- **keep** Tap the little-finger side of the right *K hand* across the index-finger side of the left *K hand*, palms facing in opposite directions.

HTML Initialism for *HyperText Markup Language.* A text-formatting language designed to transmit documents that can contain different media formats and hyper-text links to other documents; used primarily to create documents that can be seen through a browser on the World Wide Web.

■ Fingerspell: H-T-M-L

HTTP Initialism for *HyperText Transfer Protocol.* A command used on the Internet to tell the browser to look for a Web page.

■ Fingerspell: H-T-T-P

hybrid Referring to circuits that are formed by interconnecting smaller circuits of different technologies mounted together.

■ **hybrid** Beginning with both extended index fingers in front of each side of the body, palms facing down and fingers pointing forward, move hands forward toward each other, ending with the index fingers side-by-side in front of the body.

hyperlink A program device that connects computer applications and documents providing for rapid switching from one to the other.

■ **hyper-** Push the bent middle finger of the right *5 hand*, palm down, deliberately downward in front of the right side of the body.

■ **connect** Beginning with both *curved 5 hands* in front of each side of the body, palms facing each other, bring the hands together while touching the thumb and index fingertips of each hand and intersecting with each other.

hypertext[1] A nonlinear display and retrieval of information that is creatively linked, including sound, video, and graphics. When an object is selected, all of the other objects that are linked to it are listed.

■ **hyper-** Push the bent middle finger of the right *5 hand*, palm down, deliberately downward in front of the right side of the body.

■ **list**[2] Move the right *bent hand*, palm left, downward in a series of steps in front of the right side of the body.

hyper-text

hypertext[2] (alternate sign)

- **hyper-** Push the bent middle finger of the right *5 hand*, palm down, deliberately downward in front of the right side of the body.

- **blow-up** Beginning with the little-finger side of the right *S hand* on top of the index-finger side of the left *S hand*, in front of the mouth, palms facing in opposite directions, bring the hands apart while opening into *curved 5 hands* in front of each side of the head, palms facing each other.

HyperText Markup Language See sign for HTML.

HyperText Transfer Protocol See sign for HTTP.

---

icon A graphic image on a display screen that represents an application, directory, file, etc., and that can be selected with a mouse click.

- Fingerspell: I-C-O-N

- **symbol** With the index-finger side of the right *S hand*, palm forward, against the palm of the left *open hand* held in front of the chest, palm right and fingers pointing up, move both hands forward a short distance.

---

idle Referring to the time when a computer system is available for use but is not in actual operation.

- **rest** With the arms crossed at the wrists, lay the palm of each *open hand* near the opposite shoulder.

IM See sign for INSTANT MESSAGING.

---

image In computer graphics, the output form of graphics data, which is a pictorial representation of a graphics file.

- **image** Beginning with the index-finger side of the right *I hand* near the right side of the chin, palm forward, move the right hand downward, ending with the index-finger side of the right *I hand* against the palm of the left *open hand,* palm right and fingers pointing up.

---

immediate access The ability of a computer to put data in storage or remove it from storage without delay.

- **fast** Beginning with the extended index fingers of both *one hands* pointing forward in front of the chest, pull the hands back toward the chest while changing to *S hands*.

- **enter** Move the back of the right *open hand* forward in a downward arc under the palm of the left *open hand*, both palms down.

---

impact printer A printer that creates an image by striking an inked ribbon that transfers the image to the paper. A dot-matrix printer is one kind of impact printer.

■ **hit** Strike the knuckles of the right *S hand*, palm facing in, against the extended left index finger held up in front of the chest, palm facing right.

■ **print** Beginning with the thumb of the right *G hand* on the heel of the left *open hand*, tap the right index finger down to the thumb with a double movement.

■ **person marker** Move both *open hands*, palms facing each other, downward along the sides of the body.

implement To install a computer system, including choosing equipment, setting it up, and training people to use it. Related form: **implementation**.

■ **apply** Move the fingers of the right *V hand*, palm forward, downward on each side of the extended left index finger, pointing up in front of the chest.

import To bring a file created by another program into a document. See sign for DOWNLOAD. Compare UPLOAD.

increase See sign for INCREMENT.

increment, bump, or **increase** A fixed amount that is added. Related form: **incremental**.

■ **increase** Beginning with the right *U hand*, palm facing up, slightly lower than the left *U hand*, palm facing down, flip the right hand over, ending with the right fingers across the left fingers.

incremental backup See sign for ARCHIVAL BACKUP.

indent To begin or add a line or block of text so that it is set in a specific amount of space from the left or right margin.

- **indent** Move the right *B hand*, palm left, from in front of the left side of the chest to the right with a deliberate movement.

index See sign for CATALOG.

Industry Standard Architecture See sign for ISA.

information See sign for DATA[2].

information superhighway See sign for INTERNET.

initialize[1]**, install, preset,** or **setup** To prepare equipment or software for use the first time.

- **set-up** Beginning with the right *10 hand* in front of the right shoulder, palm down, twist the wrist up with a circular movement and then move the right hand straight down to land the little-finger side on the back of the left *open hand*, palm down.

initialize[2] To boot up a computer by loading the system files. Same sign used for **load**.

- **start** Beginning with the extended right index finger, palm down, inserted between the index and middle fingers of the left *open hand*, palm right and fingers pointing forward, twist the right hand, ending with palm angled forward.

- **file** Slide the little-finger side of the right *B hand*, palm angled up, between the fingers of the left *5 hand*, palm facing in, first between the index and middle fingers and then between the middle and ring fingers.

initialize[3] See signs for FORMAT[1,2,3].

initiate See sign for ACTIVATE.

ink cartridge A specific container of ink for use in ink-jet printers.

- Fingerspell: I-N-K
- **cartridge** Push the fingers of the right *bent L hand* forward a short distance in front of the chest.

ink-jet printer A printer that forms images from tiny jets of ink sprayed on the paper for high-quality printing.

- Fingerspell: I-N-K-J-E-T

  print Beginning with the thumb of the right *G hand* on the heel of the left *open hand*, tap the right index finger down to the thumb with a double movement.

- **person marker** Move both *open hands*, palms facing each other, downward along the sides of the body.

input Information that is fed into the computer for processing.

- **inside** Insert the fingertips of the right *flattened O hand*, palm down, into the center of the thumb side of the left *O hand*, palm right, with a short double movement.

input device Any equipment linked to a computer that is an entry point for feeding data, such as a keyboard, scanner, or modem.

- **inside** Insert the fingertips of the right *flattened O hand*, palm down, into the center of the thumb side of the left *O hand*, palm right, with a short double movement.

- **equipment** Move the right *E hand*, palm up, from in front of the middle of the body to the right in a double arc.

input/output device See sign for I/O DEVICE.

Input-Processing-Output-Storage cycle See sign for IPOS.

Ins See sign for INSERT KEY.

insert A text editing mode where new text pushes any existing text to the right when typed in. Compare OVERWRITE.

- **insert** Slide the little-finger side of the right *open hand*, palm in and fingers angled to the left, between the middle finger and ring finger of the left *open hand* held in front of the chest, palm right and fingers pointing up.

Insert key or **Ins** A keyboard key that switches from an overwrite mode, permitting text to be inserted without overwriting existing text.

- **insert** Slide the little-finger side of the right *open hand*, palm in and fingers angled to the left, between the middle finger and ring finger of the left *open hand* held in front of the chest, palm right and fingers pointing up.

- **key** Push the extended thumb of the right *10 hand* downward a short distance in front of the right side of the body.

install See sign for INITIALIZE[1].

instant messaging or **IM** A type of communications service that enables a user to create a private chat room with another individual.

- Fingerspell: I-M

instruction A basic command to a computer, such as to execute an operation or set a parameter.

- **teach** Move both *flattened O hands*, palms facing each other, forward with a short double movement in front of each side of the head.

instruction set A list of all the basic commands in the computer's machine language.

- **teach** Move both *flattened O hands*, palms facing each other, forward with a short double movement in front of each side of the head.

---- [sign continues] ---->

125

instruction set

- **group** Beginning with both *C hands* in front of the right side of the chest, palms facing each other, bring the hands away from each other in outward arcs while turning the palms in, ending with the little fingers near each other.

integer Any positive or negative whole number and zero, such as 52, –84, and 8. See sign for DIGIT.

intelligent terminal or **smart terminal** A terminal (monitor and keyboard) that contains memory and processing power. Compare DUMB TERMINAL.

- **smart** Bring the bent middle finger of the right *5 hand* from touching the forehead, palm in, forward while turning the palm forward.

- **terminal** Beginning with the index-finger sides of both *T hands* together in front of the chest, palms facing down, bring the hands apart to in front of each shoulder and then straight down.

Intel microprocessor The microprocessor made by Intel Corporation found in most IBM personal computers and compatibles

- Fingerspell: I-N-T-E-L
- **chip** Touch the fingertips of the right *G hand* on the palm of the left *open hand* held in front of the chest. And then twist the right hand a half turn and touch the right fingers on the left palm again.

interactive Describing a computer system that provides a means of two-way communication between the operating system and the user.

- **interact** With the thumb of the left *A hand* pointing up and the thumb of the right *A hand* pointing down, circle the thumbs around each other while moving the hands from left to right in front of the chest.

interactive program An application that responds to each user command as it is entered, then waits for the next command.

- **interact** With the thumb of the left *A hand* pointing up and the thumb of the right *A hand* pointing down, circle the thumbs around each other while moving the hands from left to right in front of the chest.

---- [sign continues] -->

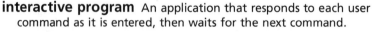

- **program** Move the middle finger of the right *P hand*, palm left, from the base to the fingertips of the left *open hand*, palm right and fingers pointing up. Repeat the movement down the back side of the left hand.

interface **1.** The connection between a computer and another entity. **2.** Software and hardware designed to allow communication between a computer and a user.

- **interface** Beginning with both *5 hands* in front of each side of the chest, fingers angled toward each other, push the hands toward each other, causing the fingers to mesh together.

internal Pertaining to a device that is built or housed inside a computer, such as an *internal modem,* an *internal speaker*, or an *internal hard drive.* Some internal devices, such as CD-ROM or floppy drives, offer access for insertion of the physical medium on the front of the case. Compare EXTERNAL.

- **in** Insert the fingertips of the right *flattened O hand,* palm down, into the center of the thumb side of the left *O hand* held in front of the chest, palm right.

internal font See sign for RESIDENT FONT.

Internet, information superhighway or **the Net**
A collection of computers all over the world that communicate with each other to send, receive, and store information.

- **Internet** Beginning with the bent middle fingers of both *5 hands* pointing toward each other in front of the chest, twist both wrists to change positions.

Internet address See sign for IP ADDRESS.

Internet Protocol See sign for IP ADDRESS.

Internet service provider See signs for ON-LINE SERVICE[1,2].

interpreter A language translator that converts a high-level programming language into machine code and runs it immediately, statement by statement.

- **interpret** With the fingertips of both *F hands* touching in front of the chest, palms facing each other, twist the hands in opposite directions to reverse positions.

---- [sign continues] --->

- **person marker** Move both *open hands*, palms facing each other, downward along the sides of the body.

---

interrupt or **trapping** A signal that causes the hardware to transfer program control to a specific location in main storage, thus breaking the normal execution of the program.

- **interrupt** Sharply tap the little-finger side of the right *open hand,* palm facing in at an angle, at the base of the thumb and index finger of the left *open hand,* with a double movement.

---

intuitive See signs for USER-FRIENDLY[1,2].

---

invoke See sign for CALL.

I/O device Acronym for *input/output device,* which is the interface of every computer that lets data move from one part to another.

- Fingerspell: I-O
- **equipment** Move the right *E hand,* palm up, from in front of the middle of the body to the right in a double arc.

IP address or **Internet address** Short for *Internet Protocol.* A number corresponding to the exact location of a computer on the Internet.

- Fingerspell: I-P
- **address** Move both *A hands,* palms facing in, upward on each side of the chest with a double movement.

IPOS cycle Acronym for *Input-Processing-Output-Storage cycle.* The transformation of data into information through input, processing, output, and storage.

- Fingerspell: I-P-O-S

ISA Acronym for *Industry Standard Architecture.* A type of expansion slot originally used in the IBM AT and still used in some modern personal computers despite the emergence of other standards.

- Fingerspell: I-S-A

ISP See signs for ON-LINE SERVICE[1,2].

italic A type style that slants text to the right.

- **italic** Beginning with both *B hands* in front of the chest, palms facing each other and fingers pointing up, bend both wrists to the right with a short double movement.

iteration Each pass through a loop. See signs for LOOP[1,2].

Java A programming language that can run on any computer connected to the Internet.
- Fingerspell: J-A-V-A

JCL Acronym for *job control language*. A language used to give instructions to the computer defining a job and the resources it requires.
- Fingerspell: J-C-L

job A task or series of tasks to be accomplished by the computer.
- **work** Tap the heel of the right *S hand,* palm forward, with a double movement on the back of the left *S hand* held in front of the body, palm down.

job control language See sign for JCL.

job queue See sign for PRIORITY PROCESSING.

Joint Photographic Experts Group See sign for JPEG.

joystick A device that can be attached to the computer to control the action of a game on the display screen.
- **joystick** With the little-finger side of the right *S hand*, palm left, in the palm of the left *open hand*, palm up, rock the right hand in different directions with a repeated movement.

JPEG (pronounced *jay-peg*) An acronym for *Joint Photographic Experts Group*. A universal graphics standard with the ability to compress images to a fraction of their original file size. Designed to replace the GIF standard, JPEG files are capable of displaying 16 million colors in a single graphic and of producing high-resolution digital photographs.
- Fingerspell: J-P-E-G

K See sign for KILOBYTE.

key[1] A button on a keyboard.
- Fingerspell: K-E-Y

key[2] (alternate sign) Same sign used for **keystroke**.
- **key** Push the extended thumb of the right *10 hand* downward a short distance in front of the right side of the body.

keyboard The set of alphanumeric, punctuation symbol, and function keys, usually in tiers, for operating a computer.
- **type** Beginning with both *5 hands* in front of the body, palms down and fingers pointing forward, wiggle the fingers with alternating movements.

- **keyboard** Beginning with the fingers of both *G hands* touching in front of the chest, palms down, move the hands away from each other to in front of each side of the chest and pinch the index fingers to the thumb of each hand.

key-field A unique field used to identify a record in a database.
- Fingerspell: K-E-Y
- **column** Move the right *G hand*, palm forward, from in front of the right shoulder downward.

keystroke The pressing of a key. See sign for KEY[2].

keyword

keyword or **descriptor** **1.** One of the significant and informative words in a title or document that describe the content of that document. **2.** A word or words in a formula that indicate the operation to be performed. **3.** A significant or informative word used to locate information on the Internet. Same sign used for **token**.

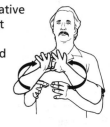

- **important** Beginning with the fingertips of both *F hands* together in front of the body, palms facing each other, bring the hands upward in an outward circular movement, ending with the index-finger sides of the *F hands* touching in front of the chest.

- **word** Touch the extended fingers of the right *G hand*, palm left, against the extended left index finger pointing up in front of the chest, palm right.

---

kilo See sign for KILOBYTE.

---

kilobyte, kilo, or **K** In binary systems, 1,024 or 2 to the 10th power.
- Fingerspell: K-B

---

label or **name** 1. A heading or description for a range of cells in a spreadsheet. 2. An identifier for a specific spot in a program. 3. A name that identifies a computer disk, a file, or a program routine.

■ **name** Tap the middle-finger side of the right *H hand* across the index-finger side of the left *H hand* with a double movement.

LAN Acronym for *Local Area Network*. A group of computers in the same vicinity connected together to share information. Compare WAN.

■ Fingerspell: L-A-N

---

language A precise way of using specific vocabulary and syntax for writing computer programs.

■ **language** Beginning with the thumbs of both *L hands* near each other in front of the chest, palms angled down, bring the hands outward with a wavy movement to in front of each side of the chest.

---

laptop computer or **notebook computer** A portable computer complete with an integrated screen and keyboard usually weighing less than 10 pounds.

■ **wallet** Beginning with the palms of both *open hands* together, right hand on top of left hand and fingers pointing in opposite directions, flip the thumb side of the right hand up while keeping the little finger on the left palm.

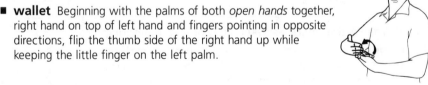

■ **computer**[1] Move the thumb side of the right *C hand,* palm left, from touching the lower part of the extended left arm upward to touch the upper arm.

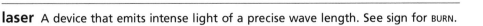

---

laser A device that emits intense light of a precise wave length. See sign for BURN.

laser printer

laser printer A type of printer that uses a laser beam to generate an image and then electronically transfers that high-quality image to paper.

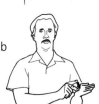

- **laser** With the index finger of the right *L hand* pointing at the palm of the left *open hand*, move the right hand back and forth with a double movement.

- **print** Beginning with the thumb of the right *G hand* on the heel of the left *open hand*, tap the right index finger down to the thumb with a double movement.

- **person marker** Move both *open hands*, palms facing each other, downward along the sides of the body.

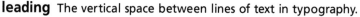

launch See sign for ACTIVATE.

layer A subset of the data in a graphics file given a logical association allowing the user to view only those parts of a drawing that are being worked on.

- **layers** Beginning with the fingers of the right *open hand* over-lapping the fingers of the left *open hand* in front of the chest, palms facing down and fingers pointing in opposite directions, reverse the position of the hands with a repeated movement as the hands move upward.

leading The vertical space between lines of text in typography.

- **leading** Place the fingertips of the right *G hand*, palm down, between the index finger and middle finger of the left *5 hand*, palm in and fingers pointing right in front of the chest.

left-justify To align text flush along the left margin.

- **left**[1] Move the left *L hand,* palm forward, from in front of the left side of the chest to the left.

---- [sign continues] ---➤

- **side** Move the left *open hand,* palm facing right and fingers pointing forward, downward in front of the left side of the chest.

length The number of characters, bytes, or bits in a computer word, whether variable or fixed.

- **length** Beginning with the extended right index finger, palm in and finger pointing down, touching the extended left index finger, palm in and finger pointing right, move the right finger outward to the right.

letter quality Used to describe printed copy of the highest quality.

- **letter** Touch the extended thumb of the right *10 hand* to the lips, palm in, and then move the thumb downward to touch the thumb of the left *10 hand* held in front of the chest, palm in.

- **quality** Shake the right *Q hand*, palm down and fingers pointing down, in front of the chest.

level The degree of subordination in a hierarchy as measured from a node to the root of a tree.

- **list**[2] Move the right *bent hand*, palm left, downward in a series of steps in front of the right side of the body.

library 1. A collection of files. 2. In programming, a collection of precompiled routines that a program can use.

- **library** Move the right *L hand,* palm forward, in a circle in front of the right shoulder.

library manager The program that maintains the programs
stored in an operating machine.

- **library** Move the right *L hand,* palm forward, in a circle in front
  of the right shoulder.

- **control** Beginning with both *modified X hands* in front of each side
  of the body, right hand forward of the left hand and palms facing
  each other, move the hands forward and back with a repeated
  movement.

- **person marker** Move both *open hands*, palms facing each other,
  downward along the sides of the body.

light pen or **electronic stylus** An input device that uses a
light-sensitive detector to select objects on a display screen.

- **light** Beginning with the fingertips of the right *8 hand* near the
  chin, palm in, flick the middle finger upward and forward with
  a double movement while opening into a *5 hand* each time.

- **write** Move the fingers of the right *modified X hand*, palm left,
  with a wiggly movement from the heel to the fingers of the left
  open hand held in front of the body.

limiting Descriptive of a device that because of its
slower speed or capacity restricts processing.
Same sign used for **parameter**.

- **limit** Beginning with both *bent hands* in front
  of the chest, right hand above the left hand
  and both palms facing down, move both
  hands forward a short distance simultaneously.

line In computer graphics, a particular set of points that when connected form a straight line.

■ **line** Beginning with the extended little fingers of both *I hands* touching in front of the chest, palms facing in, move both hands outward.

---

line up 1. A process of arranging icons on the computer's desktop in a pleasing alignment. 2. To align columns according to a specific tabular designation, such as decimal, left, or right.

■ **line-up** Beginning with the little finger of the right *4 hand*, palm left, touching the index finger of the right *4 hand*, palm right, move the right hand back toward the chest and the left hand forward.

---

link To connect two computers together through a modem, cable, or network. See sign for CONNECT.

---

link editor See signs for LINKER[1,2].

---

linker[1], link editor, or **binder** A special program that combines one or more machine-language files and converts them to a single executable file.

■ **connect** Beginning with both *curved 5 hands* in front of each side of the body, palms facing each other, bring the hands together while touching the thumb and index fingertips of each hand and intersecting with each other.

■ **change[1]** With the palm side of both *modified X hands* facing each other, twist the wrists in opposite directions in order to reverse positions.

■ **person marker** Move both *open hands*, palms facing each other, downward along the sides of the body.

linker

linker², link editor, or binder (alternate sign)

- **connect** Beginning with both *curved 5 hands* in front of each side of the body, palms facing each other, bring the hands together while touching the thumb and index fingertips of each hand and intersecting with each other.

- **person marker** Move both *open hands*, palms facing each other, downward along the sides of the body.

Linux (pronounced *linn-uks*) An operating system that is a close copy of UNIX technology, available on shareware that runs on most personal computers.

- Fingerspell: L-I-N-U-X

LISP An acronym for *List Processing*. A programming language developed in the 1960s for artificial language research.

- Fingerspell: L-I-S-P

---

list See sign for CATALOG.

List Processing See sign for LISP.

---

literal¹ A number that stays constant during programming.

- **itself** Bring the knuckles of the right *10 hand*, palm left, firmly against the side of the extended left index finger, palm right and finger pointing up in front of the chest.

- **number** Beginning with the fingertips of both *flattened O hands* touching, palms facing in opposite directions, bring the hands apart slightly while twisting the wrists in opposite directions and touch the fingertips again.

---

literal² (alternate sign)

- **letter** Touch the extended thumb of the right *10 hand* to the lips, palm in, and then move the thumb downward to touch the thumb of the left *10 hand* held in front of the chest, palm in.

load **1.** To install. **2.** To copy a program from disk storage into memory so it can be executed. Related form: **loader**. See sign for INITIALIZE[2].

local In networks, *local* refers to files, devices, and other resources at your workstation. Compare REMOTE.

- **here** Beginning with both *curved hands* in front of each side of the body, palms facing up, move the hands toward each other in repeated flat circles.

location A place in the computer's memory where information is to be stored.

- **location** Beginning with the thumbs of both *L hands* touching in front of the body, palms facing down, move the hands apart and back in a circular movement until they touch again near the chest.

lock or **lock out** To make a file, record, or other piece of data that one is working on inaccessible to other users until it is unlocked again, as in a shared database on a network.

- **lock** Beginning with the right *S hand* above the left *S hand*, both palms down, turn the right hand over, ending with the back of the right hand, palm up, on the back of the left hand, palm down.

lock out See sign for LOCK.

logical Referring to a user's perspective on the way data files or other elements in a computer system are apparently organized. For example, a single physical hard drive can be divided into two logical drives, C and D. Compare PHYSICAL, VIRTUAL.

- **logic** Move the right *L hand*, palm forward, in a double circle in front of the right side of the forehead.

logical error An error caused by a mistake in the algorithm.

- **logic** Move the right *L hand*, palm forward, in a double circle in front of the right side of the forehead.

- **wrong** Bring the middle fingers of the right *Y hand*, palm in, back against the chin with a deliberate movement.

logic construct A type of construct containing a simple sequence, condition, iteration, or case, on which all programs are based.

- **logic** Move the right *L hand,* palm forward, in a double circle in front of the right side of the forehead.

- **construct** Beginning with the fingers of the right *C hand* overlapping the fingers of the left *C hand* in front of the chest, palms facing down and fingers pointing in opposite directions, reverse the position of the hands with a repeated movement as the hands move upward.

log in, log on, or **sign on** To enter a password in order to begin a communication session with a computer, usually one used by others or one that is part of a network.

- **sign** Place the fingers of the right *H hand* firmly down on the palm of the left *open hand* held in front of the chest, palm angled right.

- **enter** Move the back of the right *open hand* forward in a downward arc under the palm of the left *open hand,* both palms down.

log off See sign for LOG OUT.

log on See sign for LOG IN.

log out, log off, or **sign out** To terminate a communication session with a computer.

- **sign** Place the fingers of the right *H hand* firmly down on the palm of the left *open hand* held in front of the chest, palm angled right.

- **disconnect** Beginning with the thumb and index fingertips of each hand intersecting, palms facing each other and right hand nearer the chest than the left hand, release the fingers and pull the left hand forward and the right hand back toward the right shoulder.

loop[1] A sequence of computer instructions that is repeatedly executed until some specified condition is met. Same sign used for **iteration**.

- **loop** Move the extended right index finger, palm down and finger pointing left, in a large circle with a double movement around the extended left index finger, palm in and finger pointing right.

loop[2] (alternate sign) Same sign used for **iteration**.

- **again** Beginning with the right *bent hand* beside the left *curved hand*, both palms up, bring the right hand up while turning it over with a double movement, ending with the fingertips of the right hand touching the palm of the left hand each time.

lowercase Small letters, as opposed to capital letters. Compare UPPERCASE.

- **small** Hold both *open hands* near each other in front of the chest, palms facing each other.

- **letter** Touch the extended thumb of the right *10 hand* to the lips, palm in, and then move the thumb downward to touch the thumb of the left *10 hand* held in front of the chest, palm in.

low-level language See signs for LOW-ORDER LANGUAGE[1,2].

low-order language[1] or **low-level language** A machine language or an assembly language. Compare HIGH-ORDER LANGUAGE.

- **low**[1] Move the right *L hand* downward in front of the right side of the chest, palm forward.

- **plan** Move both *open hands* from in front of the left side of the body, palms facing each other and fingers pointing forward, in a long smooth movement to in front of the right side of the body.

---- [sign continues] ----

low-order language

■ **language** Beginning with the thumbs of both *L hands* near each other in front of the chest, palms angled down, bring the hands outward with a wavy movement to in front of each side of the chest.

low-order language[2] or **low-level language** (alternate sign)

■ **low**[2] Move the right *open hand* downward in front of the right side of the chest, palm forward.

■ **plan** Move both *open hands* from in front of the left side of the body, palms facing each other and fingers pointing forward, in a long smooth movement to in front of the right side of the body.

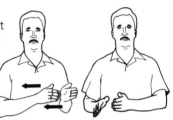

■ **language** Beginning with the thumbs of both *L hands* near each other in front of the chest, palms angled down, bring the hands outward with a wavy movement to in front of each side of the chest.

low resolution Pertaining to a low number of pixels in a picture image causing it to be less clear.

■ **not** Bring the extended thumb of the right *10 hand* from under the chin, palm left, forward with a deliberate movement.

■ **clear** Beginning with the fingertips of both *flattened O hands* touching in front of the chest, palms facing each other, move the hands quickly upward in arcs to above each shoulder while opening to *5 hands*.

---- [sign continues] ---→

■ **quality** Shake the right *Q hand*, palm down and fingers pointing down, in front of the chest.

machine address See sign for ABSOLUTE ADDRESS.

machine language Any of the lowest-level programming languages, unique to given CPUs, consisting entirely of numbers and easily understood by computers.

- **machine** With the fingers of both *curved 5 hands* loosely meshed together, palms facing in, move the hands up and down in front of the chest with a repeated movement.

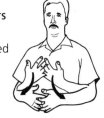

- **language** Beginning with the thumbs of both *L hands* near each other in front of the chest, palms angled down, bring the hands outward with a wavy movement to in front of each side of the chest.

machine readable Existing in a form that can be read directly into a computer by means of an input device such as a scanner.

- **machine** With the fingers of both *curved 5 hands* loosely meshed together, palms facing in, move the hands up and down in front of the chest with a repeated movement.

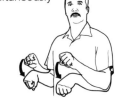

- **can** Move both *S hands,* palms facing down, downward simultaneously with a double movement in front of each side of the body.

- **read** Move the fingertips of the right *V hand*, palm down, from the fingertips to the heel of the left *open hand*, palm right.

Macintosh computer Popular family of computers manufactured by Apple Computer having an easy-to-use graphical user interface.

- Fingerspell: M-A-C

macro[1] or **shortcut key** A set of abbreviated keystrokes that activate a sequence of computer instructions. Compare HOT KEY.

- Fingerspell: M-A-C-R-O

macro[2] or **shortcut key** (alternate sign)

- **macro** Beginning with the fingertips of both *M hands* touching in front of the chest, palms facing each other, bring the hands straight apart to in front of each side of the chest.

magnetic Of or producing, caused by, or operated by magnetism.

- **magnet** Beginning with both *M hands* near each other in front of the chest, palms and fingers pointing down, swing the fingers toward each other to overlap in front of the chest with a double movement.

mail See signs for E-MAIL[1,2,3].

mailbox An area in memory or on a storage device where electronic mail is placed.

- **letter** Touch the extended thumb of the right *10 hand* to the lips, palm in, and then move the thumb downward to touch the thumb of the left *10 hand* held in front of the chest, palm in.

- **box** Beginning with both *open hands* in front of each side of the chest, palms facing each other and fingers pointing forward, move the hands deliberately in opposite directions, ending with the left hand near the chest and the right hand several inches forward of the left hand, both palms facing in.

mail list program A program that maintains names, addresses, and related data and produces mailing labels of them.

- **letter** Touch the extended thumb of the right *10 hand* to the lips, palm in, and then move the thumb downward to touch the thumb of the left *10 hand* held in front of the chest, palm in.

---- [sign continues] --->

mail list program

■ **list**[1] Touch the little-finger side of the right *bent hand*, palm in, from the fingertips of the left *open hand* down the left forearm.

■ **program** Move the middle finger of the right *P hand*, palm left, from the fingertips to the base of the left *open hand*, palm right and fingers pointing up. Repeat the movement on the back side of the left hand.

mail merge A program feature that combines names, addresses, and other data from a database with a body of prepared text in order to generate personalized form letters.

■ **letter** Touch the extended thumb of the right *10 hand* to the lips, palm in, and then move the thumb downward to touch the thumb of the left *10 hand* held in front of the chest, palm in.

■ **merge** Beginning with both *curved 5 hands* in front of each side of the chest, palms in, bring the hands together, ending with the bent fingers of both hands meshed together in front of the chest.

mainboard See signs for MOTHERBOARD[1,2].

mainframe computer or **host processor** A large computer, usually designed to serve a number of remote terminals.

■ **major** Slide the extended right index finger, palm in, from the base to the fingertip of the extended left index finger, palm right.

■ **frame** Beginning with the extended fingers of both *F hands* touching in front of the chest, palms facing each other, move the hands apart to in front of each shoulder, then straight down, and finally back together in front of the lower chest.

---- [sign continues] -->

■ **computer**[1] Move the thumb side of the right *C hand,* palm left, from touching the lower part of the extended left arm upward to touch the upper arm.

main memory See signs for RAM[1,2].

maintenance Any activity intended to eliminate faults or to keep hardware or programs in satisfactory working condition.

■ **keep** Tap the little-finger side of the right *K hand* across the index-finger side of the left *K hand*, palms facing in opposite directions.

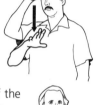

male connector A type of plug that consists of pins configured to be inserted into corresponding female connector plugs. Compare FEMALE CONNECTOR.

■ **male** Beginning with the thumb of the right *10 hand* on the right side of the forehead, bring the hand downward while opening into a *5 hand*, ending with the thumb touching the chest.

■ **plug** Move the right *V hand*, palm down, forward from in front of the right shoulder, ending with the fingers of the right *V hand* on either side of the extended left index finger held pointing up in front of the chest, palm right.

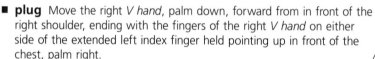

manager A person responsible for guiding the operations of a computer center, programming group, software development group, etc.

■ **control** Beginning with both *modified X hands* in front of each side of the body, right hand forward of the left hand and palms facing each other, move the hands forward and back with a repeated movement.

■ **person marker** Move both *open hands*, palms facing each other, downward along the sides of the body.

manual, operating manual, or user manual

A printed reference or tutorial book accompanying hardware or software. Compare DOCUMENTATION.

- **book** Beginning with the palms of both *open hands* together in front of the chest, fingers angled forward, bring the hands apart at the top while keeping the little fingers together.

---

map, map file, or storage map A list or file that indicates the area of storage occupied by various elements of a program and its data.

- Fingerspell: M-A-P

---

map file See sign for MAP.

---

margin The blank border around a printed page.

- **margin** Move the right *modified C hand,* palm left, downward along the little-finger side of the left *open hand,* palm facing right and fingers pointing up.

---

mark A sign or symbol used to signify or indicate an event in time or space.

- **show** With the extended right index finger touching the palm of the left *open hand,* palm right, move both hands forward a short distance.

---

mass storage[1], auxiliary storage, or secondary storage

Refers to various techniques and devices for storing large amounts of data, including floppy disks, hard disks, optical disks, and tapes.

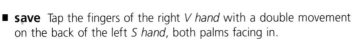

- **large** Beginning with both *L hands* from in front of each side of the chest, palms facing each other, move the hands apart.

- **save** Tap the fingers of the right *V hand* with a double movement on the back of the left *S hand,* both palms facing in.

---

mass storage², auxiliary storage, or secondary storage (alternate sign)

- **second** Beginning with the right *2 hand* in front of the right side of the chest, palm forward and fingers pointing up, twist the wrist, ending with the palm facing in.

- **save** Tap the fingers of the right *V hand* with a double movement on the back of the left *S hand*, both palms facing in.

---

match See sign for HIT.

---

maximize To increase the size of a window in a graphical user interface.

- **enlarge** Beginning with the fingertips of both *C hands* together in front of the chest, palms facing each other, pull the hands apart.

MB See sign for MEGABYTE.

---

media Plural of *medium*. There are three categories of media: source (e.g., checks), input (e.g., disks), and output (e.g., printout).

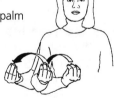

- **media** Beginning with the right *M hand* in front of the body, palm up, move the hand in a double arc to the right.

---

meg (*Informal*) See sign for MEGABYTE.

---

mega- A prefix equivalent to 2 to the 20th power in binary systems, or roughly one million.

- Fingerspell: M-E-G-A

---

megabyte, MB, or **meg** Roughly one million bytes.

- Fingerspell: M-B

megahertz or **MHz** The speed of microprocessors, the clock speed, measured in megahertz, which is approximately one million cycles per second. Compare GIGA-HERTZ.

- ■ Fingerspell: M-H-Z

---

memory The information storage inside a computer, capable of storing vast amounts of data while the computer is in use. Compare RAM[1,2].

- ■ **memory** Beginning with the fingertips of the right *curved hand* touching the right side of the forehead, palm down, bring the hand forward and down while closing the fingers into an *S hand*, palm in.

---

memory chip A semiconductor device that stores information in the form of electrical charges.

- ■ **memory** Beginning with the fingertips of the right *curved hand* touching the right side of the forehead, palm down, bring the hand forward and down while closing the fingers into an *S hand*, palm in.

- ■ **chip** Touch the fingertips of the right *G hand* on the palm of the left *open hand* held in front of the chest. And then twist the right hand a half turn and touch the right fingers on the left palm again.

---

menu, pull-down menu, or **drop-down menu** A list of options that can be called up and selected by a user, contained within a computer application.

- ■ **list**[1] Touch the little-finger side of the right *bent hand*, palm in, from the fingertips of the left *open hand* down the left forearm.

---

menu-driven interface Descriptive of a computer program that offers menus from which the user can select options for formatting or progressing.

- ■ **list**[1] Touch the little-finger side of the right *bent hand*, palm in, from the fingertips of the left *open hand* down the left forearm.

- ■ **connect** Beginning with both *curved 5 hands* in front of each side of the body, palms facing each other, bring the hands together while touching the thumb and index fingertips of each hand and intersecting with each other.

---- [sign continues] --→

- **interface** Beginning with both *5 hands* in front of each side of the chest, fingers angled toward each other, push the hands toward each other, causing the fingers to mesh together.

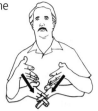

merge To combine, as two or more files or sets of database records, into a single file or database.

- **merge** Beginning with both *curved 5 hands* in front of each side of the chest, palms facing up, drop the hands down while meshing the fingers together, and then drop them apart in front of each side of the body.

message or **statement** A group of characters having meaning as a whole and always handled as a group.

- **sentence** Beginning with the thumbs and index fingers of both *F hands* touching in front of the chest, palms facing each other, pull the hands apart with a double movement, ending in front of each side of the chest.

meta or **metacharacter** A special character combination often associated with a specific key.

- Fingerspell: M-E-T-A

metalanguage A language used to describe a language. See sign for META.

method A way of doing something.

- **method** Move both *M hands* from in front of each side of the body, palms facing in and fingers angled up, downward and forward simultaneously in an arc, ending with the palms facing down and the fingers pointing down.

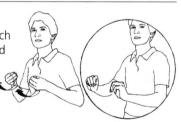

MFP See signs for MULTIFUNCTION PRINTER[1,2].

microcomputer The smallest and least expensive class of computers.

- Fingerspell: M-I-C-R-O
- **computer**[1] Move the thumb side of the right *C hand*, palm left, from touching the lower part of the extended left arm upward to touch the upper arm.

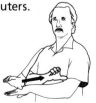

microprocessor See sign for CPU.

Microsoft A large software company that produces the Windows operating system and many application programs for personal computers and Macintosh computers.

- Fingerspell: M-S

Microsoft Disk Operating System See sign for MS-DOS.

Microsoft Windows See sign for WINDOWS.

MIDI Acronym for *musical instrument digital interface*. A standard for encoding musical sounds in digital form.

- Fingerspell: M-I-D-I

---

minimize In graphical user interfaces, to convert an open window to an icon, usually at the bottom of the display screen. Since the program is still running in the background, clicking on the icon can immediately reopen the window.

- **window** Beginning with the little-finger side of the right *B hand* on the index-finger side of the left *B hand,* both palms facing in and fingers pointing in opposite directions, move the right hand up and the left hand down simultaneously.

- **reduce** Move the right *bent hand* from in front of the chest downward to a few inches above the left *bent hand*, palms facing each other.

---

mirroring Producing graphic data that portrays an image in exactly the reverse orientation it originally had.

- **mirror** Beginning with the right *open hand* held up near the right side of the face, palm left, twist the wrist to turn the palm forward and back with a double movement.

- **image** Beginning with the index-finger side of the right *I hand* near the side of the right eye, palm forward, move the right hand downward, ending with the index-finger side of the right *I hand* against the palm of the left *open hand,* palm right and fingers pointing up.

---

mnemonic A technique used to aid human memory.

- **help** With the little-finger side of the right *A hand* in the palm of the left *open hand*, move both hands upward in front of the chest.

---- [sign continues] -->

- **remember** Move the thumb of the right *10 hand* from the right side of the forehead, palm left, smoothly down to touch the thumb of the left *10 hand* held in front of the body, palm down.

---

mnemonic code An easy-to-remember assembly language code, such as *ADD* for "addition" or *Q* for "quit."

- **easy** Brush the fingertips of the right *open hand* upward on the back of the fingertips of the left *curved hand* with a double movement, both palms up.

- **remember** Move the thumb of the right *10 hand* from the right side of the forehead, palm left, smoothly down to touch the thumb of the left *10 hand* held in front of the body, palm down.

- Fingerspell: C-O-D-E

---

mode The state or setting of a program or device, such as *insert mode* or *overstrike mode*.

- Fingerspell: M-O-D-E

---

model A complete, geometrically accurate 2-D or 3-D representation of an object on a computer graphics system that is stored in the database. Related form: **modeling.**

- **model** With the index-finger side of the right *M hand*, palm angled left, against the palm of the left *open hand*, palm angled forward, move both hands forward a short distance.

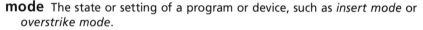

---

modem Acronym for *modulator-demodulator*. A device used by a computer to communicate to remote computers through telephone lines.

- **telephone** Bring the knuckles of the right *Y hand* in to touch the lower right cheek, holding the right thumb near the right ear and the little finger in front of the mouth.

- **connect** Beginning with both *curved 5 hands* in front of each side of the body, palms facing each other, bring the hands together while touching the thumb and index fingertips of each hand and intersecting with each other.

modify

modify To alter a program or a portion of an instruction so that the execution is changed from normal.

- **modify** Beginning with the palm sides of both *M hands* facing each other in front of the chest, twist the hands in opposite directions with a double movement.

modular Of a computer program, having a series of routines that can be programmed independently and reused. Related form: **module**.

- **groups** Beginning with both *C hands* in front of the right side of the chest, palms facing each other, bring the hands away from each other in outward arcs while turning the palms in, ending with the little fingers near each other. Repeat in front of the left side of the chest.

modulator-demodulator See sign for MODEM.

modules See sign for ROUTINE.

monitor See sign for TERMINAL.

monochrome Referring to a display screen or printer that produces only two colors, one for the foreground and one for the background.

- **one** Hold the extended index finger of the right *one hand*, palm back, in front of the right shoulder.

- **color** Wiggle the fingers of the right *5 hand* in front of the mouth, fingers pointing up and palm facing in.

motherboard[1]**, mainboard,** or **controller** The primary circuit board in a computer into which circuit cards, boards, or modules are plugged.

- **major** Slide the extended right index finger from the base to the fingertip of the index finger of the *B hand*.

---- [sign continues] --->

- **board** Bring the little-finger side of the right *B hand*, palm left, sharply against the palm of the left *C hand* held in front of the chest, palm up.

motherboard², mainboard, or controller (alternate sign)

- **control** Beginning with both *modified X hands* in front of each side of the body, right hand forward of the left hand and palms facing each other, move the hands forward and back with a repeated movement.

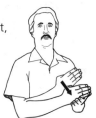

- **board** Bring the little-finger side of the right *B hand*, palm left, sharply against the palm of the left *C hand* held in front of the chest, palm up.

mouse¹ A hand-manipulated device that controls the movement of the cursor or pointer on a display screen through analogous movements on a nearby flat surface.

- **mouse¹** Move the right *modified C hand*, palm forward, around in front of the right side of the body.

mouse² (alternate sign)

- **mouse²** Flick the extended right index finger, palm facing left, across the tip of the nose with a double movement.

mousepad A pad placed on a flat surface near the display screen over which the mouse can be moved.

- **mouse¹** Move the right *modified C hand*, palm forward, around in front of the right side of the body.

---- [sign continues] ---->

mousepad

- **pad** Beginning with both extended index fingers touching in front of the body, palms down, move the fingers apart, then straight back toward the body, and then together again.

Move A command that transfers text or graphics to a new location and deletes the original.
- **move** Beginning with both *flattened O hands* in front of the body, palms down, move the hands in large arcs to the right.

MS-DOS Acronym for *Microsoft Disk Operating System*; formerly the standard operating system used by IBM-compatible personal computers.
- Fingerspell: M-S-D-O-S

multicast See sign for BROADCAST.

multifunction peripheral See signs for MULTIFUNCTION PRINTER[1,2].

multifunction printer[1], **multifunction peripheral,** or **MFP** A device that combines several functions that are normally separate, such as printing, copying, scanning, and sometimes faxing.
- Fingerspell: M-F-P

multifunction printer[2], **multifunction peripheral,** or **MFP** (alternate sign)
- **many** Beginning with both *S hands* in front of each side of the chest, palms facing in, flick the fingers open quickly into *5 hands* with a double movement.

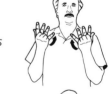

- **function** Move the fingertips of the right *F hand*, palm forward, back and forth across the index-finger side of the left *B hand*, palm in, with a double movement.

- **print** Beginning with the thumb of the right *G hand* on the heel of the left *open hand*, tap the right index finger down to the thumb with a double movement.

---- [sign continues] -->

- **person marker** Move both *open hands*, palms facing each other, downward along the sides of the body.

multimedia A combination of computer applications that use audio and video components, often in conjunction with a text document.

- **many** Beginning with both *S hands* in front of each side of the chest, palms facing in, flick the fingers open quickly into *5 hands* with a double movement.

- **movie** With the heel of the right *5 hand*, palm forward, on the heel of the left *open hand*, palm in, twist the right hand from side to side with a small repeated movement.

multiplex A computer system that manages signals between two or more devices at the same time.

- **multiplex** Beginning with the right *5 hand* in front of the chest, palm in and fingers pointing left, pull the hand to the right while changing to a *one hand*.

multiprocessing Running more than one program in a computer system at the same time, sometimes by using more than one central processing unit.

- **many** Beginning with both *S hands* in front of each side of the chest, palms facing in, flick the fingers open quickly into *5 hands* with a double movement.

- **process** Beginning with both *open hands* in front of the body, palms facing in, left fingers pointing right and right fingers pointing left, and the left hand closer to the chest than the right hand, move the left over the right hand and then the right over the left hand in an alternating movement.

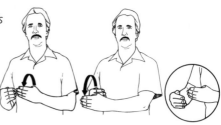

multitasking

multitasking The execution of two or more programs at the same time. Usually one of the programs is for background operations, such as printing or faxing.

■ **many** Beginning with both *S hands* in front of each side of the chest, palms facing in, flick the fingers open quickly into *5 hands* with a double movement.

■ **work** Tap the heel of the right *S hand*, palm forward, with a double movement on the back of the left *S hand* held in front of the body, palm down.

---

multithreading The ability of a computer to run different parts of one program simultaneously through a single operating system.

■ **many** Beginning with both *S hands* in front of each side of the chest, palms facing in, flick the fingers open quickly into *5 hands* with a double movement.

■ **lines** Beginning with the extended little fingers of both *I hands* touching in front of the chest, palms facing in, move the hands apart from each other to in front of each side of the chest. Repeat at a lower level in front of the body.

---

multiuser Referring to a computer system that supports more than one user working at different terminals at the same time.

■ **many** Beginning with both *S hands* in front of each side of the chest, palms facing in, flick the fingers open quickly into *5 hands* with a double movement.

■ **use** Beginning with the heel of the right *U hand* on the back of the left *S hand*, move the right hand in a small upward circle.

---- [sign continues] -->

158

■ **person marker** Move both *open hands*, palms facing each other, downward along the sides of the body.

musical instrument digital interface See sign for MIDI.

name See sign for LABEL.

name server or **domain name server** An application that maintains a table of domain names and corresponding IP addresses. Same sign used for **CSO name server**.

- **identify** Tap the thumb side of the right *I hand*, palm left, with a double movement against the left *open hand* held in front of the chest, palm forward and fingers pointing up.

- **name** Tap the middle-finger side of the right *H hand* across the index-finger side of the left *H hand* with a double movement.

- **list**[1] Touch the little-finger side of the right *bent hand*, palm in, from the fingertips of the left *open hand* down the left forearm.

nanosecond One billionth of a second. Refers to the unit of speed with which a powerful computer can execute an instruction.

- Fingerspell: N-S

natural language A spoken human language, such as English. Natural languages are not yet understood directly by a computer, although some progress has been made to enable computers and software to interpret natural-language queries.

- **natural** Move the right *N hand* in a small circle and then straight down to land on the back of the left *open hand*.

- **language** Beginning with the thumbs of both *L hands* near each other in front of the chest, palms angled down, bring the hands outward with a wavy movement to in front of each side of the chest.

navigation keys or **cursor control keys** Keyboard keys used to move the cursor around in a document.

- **click** Beginning with the right index finger pointing forward in front of the chest, bend the finger deliberately downward.

- **up**[1] Move the right extended index finger, palm forward and finger pointing up, up a short distance in front of the right side of the body.

- **down**[1] Move the right extended index finger, palm back and finger pointing down, downward a short distance in front of the right side of the body.

- **right**[1] Move the right extended index finger, palm forward and finger pointing right, to the right a short distance in front of the right side of the body.

- **left**[1] Move the right extended index finger, palm back and finger pointing left, to the left a short distance in front of the right side of the body.

near-letter quality See sign for NLQ.

nest To insert a command within another command. Related form: **nested**.

- **nest** Insert the fingers of the right *G hand*, palm left, in the thumb-side opening of the left *C hand*, palm forward.

Net, the

Net, the See sign for INTERNET.

---

network 1. A system of computers connected to each other for data transfer and communications. 2. To connect to a network.

- **network** Beginning with the bent middle fingers of both *5 hands* touching in front of the right side of the chest, palms facing in opposite directions, twist both wrists and touch again in front of the left side of the chest.

---

network computer See sign for DUMB TERMINAL.

---

network operating system The software that controls networked computers.

- **network** Beginning with the bent middle fingers of both *5 hands* touching in front of the right side of the chest, right palm angled forward and left palm facing in, twist both wrists and touch again in front of the left side of the chest.

- Fingerspell: O-S

---

network server or **file server** A computer that stores and manages programs, data, and devices for computers connected through a network.

- **network** Beginning with the bent middle fingers of both *5 hands* touching in front of the right side of the chest, right palm angled forward and left palm facing in, twist both wrists and touch again in front of the left side of the chest.

- **serve** Beginning with both *open hands* in front of each side of the body, palms facing up and right hand closer to the body than the left, move the hands forward and back with an alternating movement.

- **person marker** Move both *open hands*, palms facing each other, downward along the sides of the body.

Network Service Provider See signs for ON-LINE SERVICE[1,2].

New A command that directs the application to start a new, blank document. See sign for REFRESH.

newsgroup or **forum** A discussion area on the Internet where people can read or write their own news and messages.

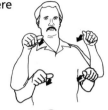

- **bulletin board** Push the thumbs of both *10 hands,* forward with a short movement, palms facing forward, first in front of each shoulder and then in front of each side of the body.

- **discuss** Tap the side of the extended right index finger, palm in, on the palm of the left *open hand*, palm up, while moving the hands to and from the chest wth a double movement.

NLQ Initialism for *near-letter quality*. Print quality that is not quite letter quality but is better than draft quality.

- Fingerspell: N-L-Q

node[1] A connection point in a network that can create, receive, or repeat a message.

- Fingerspell: N-O-D-E

node[2] or **tree structure** (alternate sign)

- **node** Beginning with the index-finger sides of both *B hands* touching in front of the chest, palms facing in and fingers pointing down, move the hands down and apart while opening the fingers to *5 hands*.

noise A disturbance that interferes with the normal operation of a computer or other device.

- **interfere** Sharply tap the little-finger side of the right *open hand*, palm facing in at an angle, at the base of the thumb and index finger of the left *open hand*, with a double movement.

NOT An operator used in programming, such as in spreadsheet formulas; used in a Boolean search to exclude an item from the search.

- **not** Bring the extended thumb of the right *10 hand* from under the chin, palm left, forward with a deliberate movement.

notation A combination of symbols, words, etc. used to designate a computer command.

- **quote** Beginning with both *bent V hands* near each side of the head, palms forward, twist the hands while bending the fingers down, ending with the palms facing back.

---

notebook computer See sign for LAPTOP COMPUTER.

NSP See signs for ON-LINE SERVICE[1,2].

---

null character A character that has a numeric value of zero but has a special meaning when interpreted as text.

- **number** Beginning with the fingertips of both *flattened O hands* touching, palms facing in opposite directions, bring the hands apart slightly while twisting the wrists in opposite directions and touch the fingertips again.

- **zero** Move both *flattened O* hands from in front of the chest outward to each side, palms facing forward.

---

number See sign for DIGIT.

---

number keypad or **numeric keypad** A set of number keys that is part of a computer keyboard.

- **number** Beginning with the fingertips of both *flattened O hands* touching, palms facing in opposite directions, bring the hands apart slightly while twisting the wrists in opposite directions and touch the fingertips again.

- **key** Push the extended thumb of the right *10 hand* downward a short distance in front of the right side of the body.

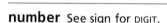

---- [sign continues] ---➤

- **pad** Beginning with both extended index fingers touching in front of the body, palms down, move the fingers apart, then straight back toward the body, and then together again.

numeric keypad See sign for NUMBER KEYPAD.

Num Lock key A keyboard key that changes the numeric keypad to cursor control mode, and vice versa.

- **number** Beginning with the fingertips of both *flattened O hands* touching, palms facing in opposite directions, bring the hands apart slightly while twisting the wrists in opposite directions and touch the fingertips again.

- **lock** Beginning with both *S hands* in front of the body, right hand above left and both palms facing down, turn the right hand over by twisting the wrist, ending with the back of the right *S hand,* palm up, on the back of the left *S hand,* palm down.

object code The version of a program that can be understood by a computer.

- **machine** With the fingers of both *curved 5 hands* loosely meshed together, palms facing in, move the hands up and down in front of the chest with a repeated movement.

- **language** Beginning with the thumbs of both *L hands* near each other in front of the chest, palms angled down, bring the hands outward with a wavy movement to in front of each side of the chest.

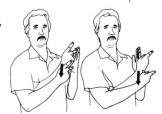

- **program** Move the middle finger of the right *P hand*, palm left, from the fingertips to the base of the left *open hand*, palm right and fingers pointing up. Repeat the movement on the back side of the left hand.

Object Linking and Embedding or **OLE** A tool used to join documents in different applications. Changes in either document are reflected in the other document.

- Fingerspell: O-L-E

---

object-oriented programming or **OOP** (see *event-driven programming*) A programming technique that creates generic building blocks of a program (the objects). The user then assembles different sets of objects as needed to solve problems.

- Fingerspell: O-O-P

OCR See sign for OPTICAL CHARACTER RECOGNITION.

---

octal or **base eight** Of or pertaining to a numbering system using a base of eight.

- **base + eight** Beginning with the right *B hand*, palm forward and fingers pointing up, under the left *open hand*, palm down and fingers pointing right, move the right hand to the right while changing into an *8 hand*.

off-line Also written **offline**. Descriptive of equipment that is not directly connected to or controlled by a computer at a given time. Same sign used for **shut down**.

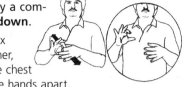

■ **disconnect** Beginning with the thumb and index fingertips of each hand intersecting with each other, palms facing each other and right hand nearer the chest than the left hand, release the fingers and pull the hands apart.

OLE See sign for OBJECT LINKING AND EMBEDDING.

OMR See sign for OPTICAL MARK READER.

on-board Available on a circuit board, such as on-board modem, on-board memory, etc.

■ **available** Move the bent middle fingertip of the right *5 hand* across the back of the left *open hand* from the wrist to off the fingertips, both palms facing down.

online or **on-line** Descriptive of equipment that is directly connected to or controlled by a computer.

■ **connect** Beginning with both *curved 5 hands* in front of each side of the body, palms facing each other, bring the hands together while touching the thumb and index fingertips of each hand and intersecting with each other.

online service[1]**, Internet service provider, ISP, Network Service Provider, NSP,** or **service provider** A for-profit provider that makes current news, stock quotes, and other information available to its subscribers over the Internet, as through a dial-up modem connection over standard telephone lines, through cable connections, or through DSL.

■ **connect** Beginning with both *curved 5 hands* in front of each side of the body, palms facing each other, bring the hands together while touching the thumb and index fingertips of each hand and intersecting with each other.

■ **serve** Beginning with both *open hands* in front of each side of the body, palms facing up and right hand closer to the body than the left, move the hands forward and back with an alternating movement.

online service², Internet Service Provider, ISP, Network Service Provider, NSP, or service provider (alternate sign)

- **serve** Beginning with both *open hands* in front of each side of the body, palms facing up and right hand closer to the body than the left, move the hands forward and back with an alternating movement.

- **provide** Beginning with both *flattened O hands* near each other in front of the chest, palms facing down, move the hands forward while turning the hands over and opening the fingers to *5 hands*.

- **person marker** Move both *open hands*, palms facing each other, downward along the sides of the body.

OOP See sign for OBJECT-ORIENTED PROGRAMMING.

---

open or **retrieve** **1.** To access a program or file. **2.** A command that opens files.

- **open** Beginning with the index-finger side of both *B hands* touching in front of the chest, palms facing forward and fingers angled up, twist both wrists while bringing the hands apart to in front of each side of the chest, ending with the palms facing in.

---

open architecture Design and structure for both computers and software whose specifications are publically available so that add-on products can be made for them.

- **open** Beginning with the index-finger side of both *B hands* touching in front of the chest, palms facing forward and fingers angled up, twist both wrists while bringing the hands apart to in front of each side of the chest, ending with the palms facing in.

- **architecture** Beginning with the thumbs of both *A hands* touching in front of the face, palms forward, move the hands apart and down a short distance at an angle, and then straight down to in front of each side of the chest.

open bus system A bus system that has expansion slots on the motherboard.

- **open** Beginning with the index-finger side of both *B hands* touching in front of the chest, palms facing forward and fingers angled up, twist both wrists while bringing the hands apart to in front of each side of the chest, ending with the palms facing in.

- **bus** Beginning with the little-finger side of the right *B hand* touching the index-finger side of the left *B hand,* palms facing in opposite directions, move the right hand back toward the right shoulder.

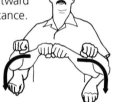

- **system** Beginning with the index-finger sides of both *S hands* touching in front of the chest, palms down, move the hands outward to in front of each shoulder and then straight down a short distance.

operating manual See sign for MANUAL.

operating system[1] or **OS** A group of programs that help the computer's components function together smoothly.

- Fingerspell: O-S

operating system[2] or **OS** (alternate sign)

- **run** Brush the palm of the right *open hand* upward with a double movement on the palm of the left *open hand* held up in front of the chest.

- **system** Beginning with the index-finger sides of both *S hands* touching in front of the chest, palms down, move the hands outward to in front of each shoulder and then straight down a short distance.

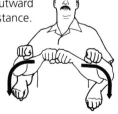

169

operation A defined action specified by a single computer instruction. Same sign used for **action, performance**. Related forms: **operate, operational**.

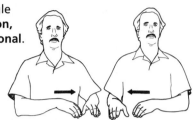

- **do** Move both *C hands,* palms facing down, simultaneously back and forth in front of the body with a swinging movement.

---

optical character recognition or **OCR** A program that translates graphics images of letters and numbers to character bits that can be manipulated by a word processor, spreadsheet, or other similar program.

- **character** Move the right *C hand,* palm left, in a small circle and then back against the left side of the chest.

- **recognize** Bring the extended curved right index finger from touching the cheek near the right eye, palm left, downward to touch the palm of the left *open hand,* palm right in front of the chest.

---

optical disk drive A large-capacity data storage medium for computers, on which information is stored at extremely high density in the form of tiny pits.

- **bar** Move the fingers of the right *G hand*, palm forward, from left to right in front of the chest.

- **read** Move the fingertips of the right *V hand*, down across the palm of the left *open hand* with a double movement.

- **person marker** Move both *open hands*, palms facing each other, downward along the sides of the body.

optical mark reader or **OMR** A reader that senses magnetized marks made by the magnetic particles in lead from a pencil.

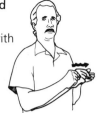

- **write** Move the fingers of the right *modified X hand*, palm left, with a wiggly movement from the heel to the fingers of the left *open hand* held in front of the body.

- **recognize** Bring the extended curved right index finger from touching the cheek near the right eye, palm left, downward to touch the palm of the left *open hand,* palm right in front of the chest.

optical scanner See sign for SCANNER.

options Choices available to the user, such as how a program is to look on the display screen, whether to periodically save active documents, etc. Same sign used for **select**.

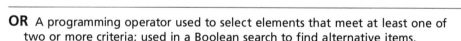

- **choose** Beginning with the bent thumb and index finger of the right *5 hand* touching the index finger of the left *V hand*, palms facing each other, pull the right hand back toward the right shoulder while pinching the thumb and index finger together. Repeat from the middle finger of the left *V hand*.

OR A programming operator used to select elements that meet at least one of two or more criteria; used in a Boolean search to find alternative items.

- Fingerspell: O-R

order See sign for SEQUENTIAL.

OS See signs for OPERATING SYSTEM[1,2].

output 1. Anything, whether meaningful data or garbled nonsense, sent out from a computer, as to a display monitor or printer. 2. Having to do with the transfer of data.

- **out** Beginning with the fingertips of the right *flattened O hand*, palm down, inserted in the thumb-side opening of the left *flattened O hand*, palm in, bring the right hand upward in an arc to the right while opening into a *flattened C hand*, palm left.

overflow condition See sign for OVERFLOW ERROR.

overflow error

overflow error or **overflow condition** A condition occurring when the available data is greater than the space allocated to hold it, causing loss of data or incorrect results in computations.

- **overflow** Slide the fingers of the right *open hand*, palm forward, over the index-finger side of the left *flattened O hand*, palm in, while opening into a *5 hand* as it goes over to the back of the left hand.

- **wrong** Bring the middle fingers of the right *Y hand*, palm in, back against the chin with a deliberate movement.

overlay or **cascade** A command to arrange open windows on the display screen so that they overlap each other.

- **overlay** Beginning with the right *open hand*, palm down, in front of the right side of the chest, move the hand forward in an arc to land across the back of the left *open hand* held in front of the chest, palm down.

overtype See sign for OVERWRITE.

overwrite or **overtype** A text editing mode where typed-in new text replaces existing text instead of pushing the existing text along. Compare INSERT.

- **type** Beginning with both *5 hands* in front of the body, palms down and fingers pointing forward, wiggle the fingers with alternating movements.

- **on** Bring the palm of the right *open hand* downward on the back of the left *open hand* held in front of the body, both palms facing down.

---

pack¹ To store several units of data together on disk, especially in a compressed format. Compare <small>UNPACK</small>. Related form: **packed**.

- **pack¹** Beginning with the right *S hand*, palm in, above the palm of the left *open hand*, palm up, move both hands upward in front of the chest.

---

pack² (alternate sign) Related form: **packed**.

- **pack²** Beginning with the right *P hand*, palm down, over the palm of the left *open hand*, palm up, move the right hand in a double circular movement.

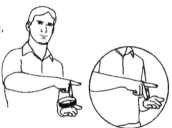

---

pack³ (alternate sign) Related form: **packed**.

- **pack³** Beginning with the thumb of the right *C hand*, palm left, on the palm of the left *open hand*, palm up, bring the right fingers downward to form a *flattened C hand*.

---

packet A small block of data with an address for transmission with other packets over a modem.

- **packet** Beginning with both *G hands* in front of the left side of the chest, palms facing each other and fingertips touching, bring the hands away from each other in outward arcs while turning the palms in, ending the with the little fingers touching. Repeat in front of the chest and again in front of the right side of the chest.

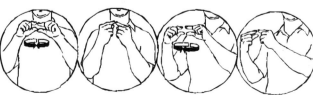

page **1.** A single sheet of data in a word processing program or delivered as output from a printer. **2.** The unit of program or data swapped back and forth from virtual memory to main memory.

■ **page** Strike the extended thumb of the right *10 hand*, palm down, against the left open palm with a double upward movement.

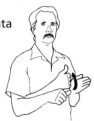

page break The end of a single page of text, set up so that a page-break code will be inserted after a certain number of lines as a default for an entire document or file, or so that it is inserted by a special user command.

■ **page** Strike the extended thumb of the right *10 hand*, palm down, against the left open palm with a double upward movement.

■ **end** Move the palm side of the right *open hand*, palm left and fingers pointing forward, deliberately down past the fingertips of the left *open hand*, palm in and fingers pointing right.

Page Down A keyboard key that moves the cursor down a set number of lines equivalent to either the exact length of a printed page or the length of a full screen.

■ **page** Strike the extended thumb of the right *10 hand*, palm down, against the left open palm with a double upward movement.

■ **down**[1] Move the right extended index finger, palm back and finger pointing down, downward a short distance in front of the right side of the body.

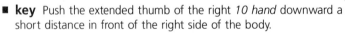

■ **key** Push the extended thumb of the right *10 hand* downward a short distance in front of the right side of the body.

Page Up A keyboard key that moves the cursor up a set number of lines equivalent to either the exact length of a printed page or the length of a full screen.

■ **page** Strike the extended thumb of the right *10 hand*, palm down, against the left open palm with a double upward movement.

■ **up**[1] Move the right extended index finger, palm forward and finger pointing up, up a short distance in front of the right side of the body.

■ **key** Push the extended thumb of the right *10 hand* downward a short distance in front of the right side of the body.

pagination The numbering of printed pages in a document.

■ **page** Strike the extended thumb of the right *10 hand*, palm down, against the left open palm with a double upward movement.

■ **number** Beginning with the fingertips of both *flattened O hands* touching, palms facing in opposite directions, bring the hands apart slightly while twisting the wrists in opposite directions and touch the fingertips again.

palette A complete set of available colors in a computer graphics system.

■ **color** Wiggle the fingers of the right *5 hand* in front of the mouth, fingers pointing up and palm facing in.

---- [sign continues] --➤

palette

- **square** With both extended index fingers, palms down, trace a square in the air, beginning together in front of the chest, moving apart to each side, moving then straight down, and then together again at the bottom.

palmtop computer, picocomputer, or handheld computer
A reduced-size computer having reduced capabilities that fits in the user's hand.

- **palm-size** Move the fingertips of the right *C hand* down the palm of the left *open hand* held in front of the chest.

- **computer**[1] Move the thumb side of the right *C hand*, palm left, from touching the lower part of the extended left arm upward to touch the upper arm.

paper feed or sheet feeder The method by which paper is pulled through a printer.

- **paper** Brush the heel of the right *open hand*, with a double movement on the heel of the left *open hand*, palms facing each other.

- **feed** Push both *flattened O hands*, palms facing up and fingers pointing forward, one hand somewhat forward of the other hand, forward with a short double movement.

paragraph A unit of text that begins and ends with the Enter keystroke.

- **paragraph** Tap the fingertips of the right *C hand* against the palm of the left *open hand* held in front of the chest, palm right and fingers pointing up.

parallel Descriptive of operations that occur simultaneously or side by side.

- **parallel** Beginning with both extended index fingers in front of the chest, palms facing down and index fingers pointing forward, move the hands forward simultaneously.

parallel interface A channel capable of transferring eight bits of data simultaneously.

- **parallel** Beginning with both extended index fingers in front of the chest, palms facing down and index fingers pointing forward, move the hands forward simultaneously.

- **interface** Beginning with both *5 hands* in front of each side of the chest, fingers angled toward each other, push the hands toward each other, causing the fingers to mesh.

parallel port An interface for connecting an external device such as a parallel printer.

- **parallel** Beginning with both extended index fingers in front of the chest, palms facing down and index fingers pointing forward, move the hands forward simultaneously.

- **connect** Beginning with both *curved 5 hands* in front of each side of the body, palms facing each other, bring the hands together while touching the thumb and index finger-tips of each hand and intersecting with each other.

parameter A limit or characteristic of, as of a particular program or computer operating system. See sign for LIMITING.

partition The division of a large hard disk into smaller segments for more efficient management of programs and data. See sign for ALLOCATE[1].

Pascal

Pascal A programming language developed in the 1970s used for teaching programming concepts.

- Fingerspell: P-A-S-C-A-L

pass See sign for CYCLE.

password[1] or **access code** A secret series of characters that enables a user to access a file, computer, or program, and that is intended to prevent access by unauthorized users.

- **private** Tap the thumb side of the right *A hand*, palm left, against the mouth with a repeated movement.

- **word** Touch the extended fingers of the right *G hand*, palm left, against the extended left index finger pointing up in front of the chest, palm right.

password[2] or **access code** (alternate sign)

- **enter** Move the back of the right *open hand* forward in a downward arc under the palm of the left *open hand*, both palms down.

- **private** Tap the thumb side of the right *A hand*, palm left, against the mouth with a repeated movement.

- **word** Touch the extended fingers of the right *G hand*, palm left, against the extended left index finger pointing up in front of the chest, palm right.

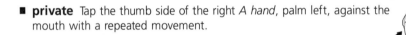

Paste A command to place information previously "Cut" from a document into a new position or a different document. Compare CUT-AND-PASTE.

- **paste-up** Beginning with the thumbs of both *10 hands* touching in front of the chest, palms facing down, bring the hands downward and apart with a double movement by twisting the wrists.

path A list of directories where the operating system looks for executable files. Same sign used for **routing**.

- **road** Move both *open hands* from in front of each side of the body, palms facing each other, forward with a parallel movement.

PC See signs for DESKTOP COMPUTER[1,2].

PCI Initialism for *Peripheral Component Interconnect.* A type of expansion slot connected directly with the microprocessor, making it one of the fastest ways to connect a hard disk controller, video card, or network interface to a computer.

- Fingerspell: P-C-I

PCMCIA Initialism for *Personal Computer Memory Card International Association.* An organization responsible for establishing the standard for a credit-card size, metal expansion card for laptop and some other computers.

- Fingerspell: P-C-M-C-I-A

Pentium processor A 32-bit micro-processor introduced by Intel in 1993.

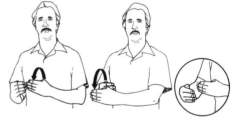

- Fingerspell: P-E-N-T-I-U-M

- **process** Beginning with both *open hands* in front of the body, palms facing in, left fingers pointing right and right fingers pointing left, and the left hand closer to the chest than the right hand, move the left over the right hand and then the right over the left hand in an alternating movement.

performance A major factor in determining the total productivity of a system as determined by a combination of availability, throughput, and response time. See sign for OPERATION.

performance monitor A program used to keep track of a computer's performance by monitoring the service levels of what is being delivered from various hardware devices.

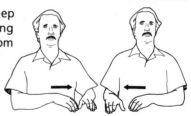

- **do** Move both *C hands*, palms facing down, simultaneously back and forth in front of the body with a swinging movement.

- **monitor** Beginning with both *V hands* in front of the body, palms facing down and fingers pointing forward, move the hands in a circular movement in front of the body with a simultaneous double movement.

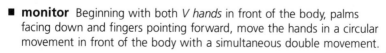

179

peripheral

peripheral[1] Short for *peripheral device*. Any external equipment that is connected to a computer, such as a printer or scanner.

- **connect-connect** Beginning with both *curved 5 hands* in front of the left side of the body, palms facing each other, bring the hands together while touching the thumb and index fingertips of each hand and intersecting with each other. Repeat in front of the right side of the body.

- **equipment** Move the right *E hand,* palm up, from in front of the middle of the body to the right in a double arc.

peripheral[2] (alternate sign)

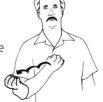

- **peripheral** Move the extended middle finger of the right *P hand*, palm down, in a circle around the fingertips of the left *B hand*, palm in and fingers pointing up.

Peripheral Component Interconnect See sign for PCI.

peripheral device See signs for PERIPHERAL[1,2].

personal computer See signs for DESKTOP COMPUTER[1,2].

Personal Computer Memory Card International Association See sign for PCMCIA.

phase conversion The changing of existing data files to a new format by implementing the new system one part at a time.

- **parts** Slide the little-finger side of the right *open hand,* palm left, with a double movement across the palm of the left *open hand,* palm up, moving to a different section of the left hand each time.

- **convert**[1] With both *C hands* in front of the chest, thumbs touching, turn the right hand down and back up again.

physical Referring to hardware rather than software. Compare
LOGICAL, VIRTUAL.

- **physical** Touch the palm side of both *P hands,* palms facing in and fingers pointing toward each other, first on each side of the chest and then on each side of the waist.

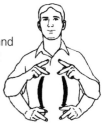

picocomputer See sign for PALMTOP COMPUTER.

Picture Element See sign for PIXEL.

pipelining A design that provides two or more processing pathways that can be used simultaneously.

- **pipeline** Move both *5 hands* forward from in front of the body, palms facing down and fingers pointing forward.

piracy or **software piracy** The process of copying commercial software without the permission of the developer.

- **steal** Beginning with the index-finger side of the right *V hand*, palm down, on the elbow of the bent left arm, held at an upward angle across the chest, pull the right hand upward toward the left wrist while bending the fingers in tightly.
- Fingerspell: S-W

pitch The number of characters printed per inch in word processing when using a monospaced font.

- Fingerspell: P-I-T-C-H

pixel Short for *Picture Element*, which is a single point and the smallest element in a graphic image.

- Fingerspell: P-I-X-E-L

place marker See sign for BOOKMARK.

platform The underlying hardware and operating system software for a system.

- **floor** Beginning with the index-finger side of both *B hands* touching in front of the waist, palms facing down and fingers pointing forward, move the hands apart to each side.

---- [sign continues] ---->

platform

- **environment** Move the right *E hand* in a circle around the extended left index finger, palm right and finger pointing up.

---

plot[1] To produce an image by drawing lines on a display screen or on paper.

- **plot**[1] Move the extended middle finger of the right *P hand* from the heel to off the fingertips of the upturned left *open hand*.

---

plot[2] (alternate sign)

- **plot**[2] Move the right *X hand*, palm forward, from in front of the left side of the chest in an up and down movement to in front of the right side of the chest.

---

plotter A printing device that produces high-quality output charts and graphs by moving ink pens over the surface of the paper.

- **plot**[2] Move the right *X hand*, palm forward, from in front of the left side of the chest in an up and down movement to in front of the right side of the chest.

- **print** Beginning with the thumb of the right *G hand* on the heel of the left *open hand*, tap the right index finger down to the thumb with a double movement.

- **person marker** Move both *open hands*, palms facing each other, downward along the sides of the body.

---

plug A connector on a cable used to link devices together.

- **plug** Move the right *V hand*, palm down, forward from in front of the right shoulder, ending with the fingers of the right *V hand* on either side of the extended left index finger held pointing up in front of the chest, palm right.

Plug and Play Technology jointly developed by Intel Corporation and Microsoft and designed so that all a user needs to do is plug in a peripheral. The computer system will configure it automatically, and it will be ready to work.

- **plug** Move the right *V hand*, palm down, forward from in front of the right shoulder, ending with the fingers of the right *V hand* on either side of the extended left index finger held pointing up in front of the chest, palm right.

- **and** Move the right *5 hand*, palm in and fingers pointing left, from in front of the left side of the body to the right while closing the fingers to a *flattened O hand*.

- **play** Swing both *Y hands* up and down by twisting the wrists in front of each side of the body with a repeated movement.

point and click The technique used in graphical user interfaces for selecting an object by moving the mouse cursor to it, then pressing and releasing the mouse button.

- **period** With the right index finger and thumb pinched together, palm forward, push the right hand forward a short distance.

- **click** Beginning with the right index finger pointing forward in front of the chest, bend the finger deliberately downward.

polling Making continuous requests from other devices to see if there is information to send. Related form: **poll**.

- ■ **test** Beginning with both extended index fingers pointing forward in front of the chest, palms down, bring the hands downward while bending the index fingers into *X hands* and continuing down while extending the index fingers again.

---

pop or **pull** Pulling one item off a stack of items in a program push-down list or making it the topmost item. Compare PUSH.

- ■ **appear** With a double movement, push the extended right index finger, palm left, upward between the index finger and middle finger of the left *open hand*, palm down.

---

pop-up window A window that suddenly appears when an option is selected with a mouse or with a special function key.

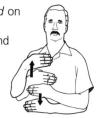

- ■ **appear** With a double movement, push the extended right index finger, palm left, upward between the index finger and middle finger of the left *open hand*, palm down.

- ■ **window** Beginning with the little-finger side of the right *B hand* on the index-finger side of the left *B hand*, both palms facing in and fingers pointing in opposite directions, move the right hand up and the left hand down simultaneously.

---

port An interface on a computer to which peripheral devices are connected, such as printers and monitors.

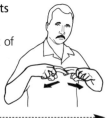

- ■ **port** Touch the fingertips of the right *G hand*, palm left, against the palm of the left *open hand*, palm right and fingers pointing up.

---

post See sign for BULLETIN BOARD[1].

---

postmortem Pertaining to the analysis of an operation after its completion.

- ■ **analyze** With both *V hands* pointing toward each other in front of the chest, palms down, move the fingers down and apart with a double movement, bending the fingers each time.

---- [sign continues] -->

- **after** Push the little-finger side of the right *B hand* over the index-finger side of the left *B hand* held in front of the chest, palm in and fingers pointing right.

power down To turn a machine off. Same sign used for **power up**.

- **turn off** While holding an imaginary switch between the thumb and bent index finger of the right *X hand* held in front of the right side of the body, palm up, twist the wrist, ending with the palm facing down.

power supply A device that converts AC power to low-level DC power for a computer.

- **electric** Tap the knuckles of the index fingers of both *X hands* together, palms facing in, with a double movement.

- **feed** Push both *flattened O hands*, palms facing up and fingers pointing forward, one hand somewhat forward of the other hand, forward with a short double movement.

power surge A sudden increase in line voltage that can damage computer hardware and software. Compare SURGE.

- **electric** Tap the knuckles of the index fingers of both *X hands* together, palms facing in, with a double movement.

- **hit** Strike the knuckles of the right *S hand,* palm facing in, against the extended left index finger held up in front of the chest, palm facing right.

power up To turn a machine on. See sign for POWER DOWN.

precision The degree of detail with which a quantity is stated. See sign for ACCURACY.

preset

preset See sign for INITIALIZE[1].

primary memory See signs for RAM[1,2].

print **1.** A keyboard command to send a screen, page, multiple pages, or a file to a printer output device. **2.** To generate a hard copy of a document or file. **3.** The BASIC language command that displays information on-screen.

- **print** Beginning with the thumb of the right *G hand* on the heel of the left *open hand*, tap the right index finger down to the thumb with a double movement.

printer A device that prints text or illustrations on paper.

- **print** Beginning with the thumb of the right *G hand* on the heel of the left *open hand*, tap the right index finger down to the thumb with a double movement.

- **person marker** Move both *open hands*, palms facing each other, downward along the sides of the body.

printer driver A file containing the information that a program needs in order to print on a given brand and model of printer.

- **print** Beginning with the thumb of the right *G hand* on the heel of the left *open hand*, tap the right index finger down to the thumb with a double movement.

- **person marker** Move both *open hands*, palms facing each other, downward along the sides of the body.

- Fingerspell: D-R-I-V-E-R

printer server See sign for SERVER.

printout Computer output printed on paper.

- **print** Beginning with the thumb of the right *G hand* on the heel of the left *open hand*, tap the right index finger down to the thumb with a double movement.

- **out** Beginning with the right *flattened O hand* inserted in the palm side of the left *C hand*, bring the right hand upward.

priority processing or **job queue** The processing of a sequence of jobs on the basis of assigned priorities.

- **priority** Touch the middle finger of the right *P hand*, palm in, first to the thumb, then in order to each finger of the left *5 hand* held in front of the body, palm in and fingers pointing up.

- **process** Beginning with both *open hands* in front of the body, palms facing in, left fingers pointing right and right fingers pointing left, and the left hand closer to the chest than the right hand, move the left over the right hand and then the right over the left hand in an alternating movement.

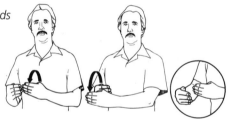

privacy The ability to protect those personal aspects a person chooses to shield from public scrutiny, like a Social Security number or a password. Related form: **private**.

- **private** Tap the thumb side of the right *A hand*, palm left, against the mouth with a repeated movement.

privileged instruction A computer instruction not available for use in ordinary programs written by users.

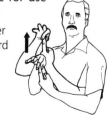

- **special** Grasp the left extended index finger, palm in and finger pointing up, with the fingers of the right *G hand* and pull upward in front of the chest.

---- [sign continues] ------------------>

- **teach** Move both *flattened O hands*, palms facing each other, forward with a short double movement in front of each side of the head.

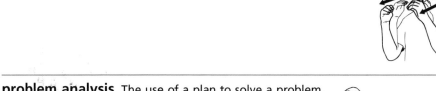

problem analysis The use of a plan to solve a problem, which is the first step in the program developmental cycle.

- **problem** Beginning with the knuckles of both *bent V hands*, touching in front of the chest, twist the hands in opposite directions with a deliberate movement, rubbing the knuckles against each other.

- **analyze** With both *V hands* pointing toward each other in front of the chest, palms down, move the fingers down and apart with a double movement, bending the fingers each time.

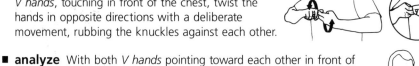

procedural, process, or **processing** The steps that must be followed to accomplish a specific computer-related task. Related form: **procedure**.

- **process** Beginning with both *open hands* in front of the body, palms facing in, left fingers pointing right and right fingers pointing left, and the left hand closer to the chest than the right hand, move the left over the right hand and then the right over the left hand in an alternating movement.

process See sign for PROCEDURAL. Related form: **processing**.

processor See sign for CPU.

program See signs for DEVELOP, APPLICATION.

program file A file containing instructions written in a programming language to tell the computer what to do.

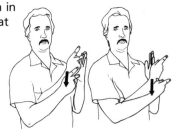

- **program** Move the middle finger of the right *P hand*, palm left, from the fingertips to the base of the left *open hand*, palm right and fingers pointing up. Repeat the movement on the back side of the left hand.

---- [sign continues] --->

- **file** Slide the little-finger side of the right *B hand,* palm angled up, between the fingers of the left *5 hand,* palm facing in, first between the index and middle fingers and then between the middle and ring fingers.

programmable Capable of being controlled through instructions altered or manipulated by the user.

- **program** Move the middle finger of the right *P hand,* palm left, from the fingertips to the base of the left *open hand,* palm right and fingers pointing up. Repeat the movement on the back side of the left hand.

- **can** Move both *S hands,* palms facing down, downward simultaneously with a double movement in front of each side of the body.

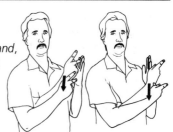

programmable read-only memory or **PROM** A read-only memory chip programmed at the factory for use with a given computer.

- Fingerspell: P-R-O-M

Program Manager The main interface helping users navigate original versions of Windows.

- **program** Move the middle finger of the right *P hand,* palm left, from the fingertips to the base of the left *open hand,* palm right and fingers pointing up. Repeat the movement on the back side of the left hand.

- **control** Beginning with both *modified X hands* in front of each side of the body, right hand forward of the left hand and palms facing each other, move the hands forward and back with a repeated movement.

---- [sign continues] -->

Program Manager

- **person marker** Move both *open hands*, palms facing each other, downward along the sides of the body.

programmer A person trained in the use of a programming language who creates, tests, and documents computer programs.

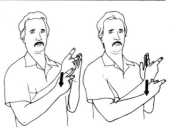

- **program** Move the middle finger of the right *P hand*, palm left, from the fingertips to the base of the left *open hand*, palm right and fingers pointing up. Repeat the movement on the back side of the left hand.

- **person marker** Move both *open hands*, palms facing each other, downward along the sides of the body.

programming The creation of a list of stored instructions that tell the computer what to do. See sign for APPLICATION.

programming language A high level language consisting of vocabulary and syntax for writing instructions for the computer.

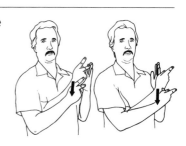

- **program** Move the middle finger of the right *P hand*, palm left, from the fingertips to the base of the left *open hand*, palm right and fingers pointing up. Repeat the movement on the back side of the left hand.

- **language** Beginning with the thumbs of both *L hands* near each other in front of the chest, palms angled down, bring the hands outward with a wavy movement to in front of each side of the chest.

project An undertaking, having a definite objective and specific start and completion point, with tasks and activities set up in logical order to achieve the objective.

- **project** Move the middle finger of the right *P hand*, palm left, from the fingertips to the base of the left *open hand*, palm right and fingers pointing up. Then move the right extended little finger in an arc from the fingertips to the base of the back side of the left hand.

PROM See sign for PROGRAMMABLE READ-ONLY MEMORY.

prompt See sign for CURSOR.

proof See sign for VERIFY.

proprietary or **closed architecture** Hardware or software that is privately owned and is sold with the understanding that the seller retains ownership and the buyer purchases only the right of usage as outlined in a licensing agreement. Compare OPEN ARCHITECTURE.

- **private** Tap the thumb side of the right *A hand*, palm left, against the mouth with a repeated movement.

- **own** Beginning with the right *5 hand* in front of the chest, palm forward, bring the hand back to the chest while closing the fingers forming a *flattened O hand*.

protect To prevent unauthorized access to programs or a computer system.

- **protect** With the wrists of both *S hands* crossed in front of the chest, palms facing in opposite directions, move the hands forward with a short double movement.

protected field A block of test, a formula, etc. that cannot be altered or overwritten.

- **column** Move the right *modified C hand*, palm forward, from in front of the right shoulder downward.

---- [sign continues] --------->

protected field

- **protect** With the wrists of both *S hands* crossed in front of the chest, palms facing in opposite directions, move the hands forward with a short double movement.

- **can't** Bring the extended index finger of the right *one hand* downward, hitting the extended index finger of the left *one hand* as it moves.

- **change**[1] With the palm side of both *modified X hands* facing each other, twist the wrists in opposite directions in order to reverse positions.

protected files or read-only files Files that are safeguarded so that they can be read but not altered.

- **file** Slide the little-finger side of the right *B hand,* palm angled up, between the fingers of the left *5 hand,* palm facing in, first between the index and middle fingers and then between the middle and ring fingers.

- **protect** With the wrists of both *S hands* crossed in front of the chest, palms facing in opposite directions, move the hands forward with a short double movement.

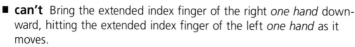

- **can't** Bring the extended index finger of the right *one hand* downward, hitting the extended index finger of the left *one hand* as it moves.

---- [sign continues] ------------------------------>

- **change**[1] With the palm side of both *modified X hands* facing each other, twist the wrists in opposite directions in order to reverse positions.

protocol A set of standards for exchanging information.

- **policy** Touch the index-finger side of the right *P hand*, palm down, first against the fingers and then against the heel of the left *open hand*, palm forward and fingers pointing up.

proxy server A server that acts as a security measure to enable users behind a firewall to browse the Web without exposing the proprietary contents that the firewall is protecting to public scrutiny.

- Fingerspell: P-R-O-X-Y

- **safe** Beginning with both *S hands* crossed at the wrists in front of the chest, palms facing in opposite directions, twist the wrists and move the hands apart, ending with the hands in front of each shoulder, palms facing forward.

- **serve** Beginning with both *open hands* in front of each side of the body, palms facing up and right hand closer to the body than the left, move the hands forward and back with an alternating movement.

- **person marker** Move both *open hands*, palms facing each other, downward along the sides of the body.

pseudocode Created in the 1970s as an alternative to flowcharts, a stylized form of writing used to describe the logic of a program.

- **fake** Beginning with the index finger of the right *4 hand* touching the right side of the forehead, move the hand forward in several short movements.

- Fingerspell: C-O-D-E

publish a message

publish a message See sign for BULLETIN BOARD[1].

pull See sign for POP.

pull-down menu See sign for MENU.

purge See sign for CLEAR[1].

push In programming, to place a data item onto a stack. Compare POP.

- **on-to** Bring the palm of the right *open hand* downward on the back of the left *open hand* held in front of the body, both palms facing down.

push-down list A list written from the bottom up, with each new entry placed on the top of the list.

- **layers** Beginning with the fingers of the right *open hand* overlapping the fingers of the left *open hand* in front of the chest, palms facing down and fingers pointing in opposite directions, reverse the position of the hands with a repeated movement as the hands move upward.

- **list**[1] Touch the little-finger side of the right *bent hand*, palm in, from the fingertips of the left *open hand* down the left forearm.

quality control A technique for evaluating the quality of a product being processed by checking it against a predetermined standard.

■ **quality** Shake the right *Q hand*, palm down and fingers pointing down, in front of the chest.

■ **analyze** With both *V hands* pointing toward each other in front of the chest, palms down, move the fingers down and apart with a double movement, bending the fingers each time.

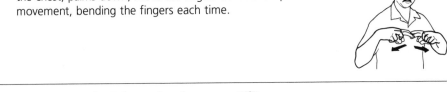

query A request for information from a database.

■ **query** Beginning with both extended index fingers pointing up in front of each side of the chest, palms forward, move the right hand down while bending into an *X hand* and then the left hand down while bending into an *X hand*, ending with both *X hands* in front of the chest.

question mark A character used to show an omission of a single character in a search string. See sign for WILDCARD[2].

queue A group of items waiting to be acted upon by the computer.

■ **line-up** Beginning with the little finger of the right *4 hand*, palm left, touching the index finger of the right *4 hand*, palm right, move the right hand back toward the chest and the left hand forward.

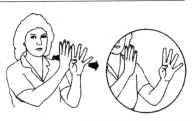

QuickTime A program for storing and displaying digital video.

■ **fast** Beginning with the extended index fingers of both *one hands* pointing forward in front of the chest, pull the hands back toward the chest while changing to *S hands*.

---- [sign continues] --➤

195

QuickTime

- **time** Tap the bent index finger of the right *X hand*, palm down, with a double movement on the wrist of the downturned left hand.

quit See signs for ESCAPE[1,2].

RAM[1], main memory, or **primary memory** Acronym for *random-access memory*. The computer's main working memory where program instructions and data are stored while the computer is running so that they can be directly accessed by the central processing unit through the processor's high-speed data bus.

- Fingerspell: R-A-M

RAM[2], main memory, or **primary memory** (alternate sign)

- **specialized** Slide the extended right index finger from the base to the fingertip of the index finger of the left *B hand*, palm right.

- **memory** Beginning with the fingertips of the right *curved hand* touching the right side of the forehead, palm down, bring the hand forward and down while closing the fingers into an *S hand*, palm in.

random Something occurring without a plan or pattern.

- **random** Beginning with the extended fingers of both *R hands* touching in front of the chest, palms facing down, move the hands apart to in front of each shoulder with a wavy movement.

random access See sign for DIRECT ACCESS.

random access memory See signs for RAM[1,2].

random processing or **direct-access processing** Processing of data in any order. Compare SEQUENTIAL PROCESSING.

- **random** Beginning with the extended fingers of both *R hands* touching in front of the chest, palms facing down, move the hands apart to in front of each shoulder with a wavy movement.

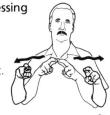

---- [sign continues] -->

197

random processing

■ **process** Beginning with both *open hands* in front of the body, palms facing in, left fingers pointing right and right fingers pointing left, and the left hand closer to the chest than the right hand, move the left over the right hand and then the right over the left hand in an alternating movement.

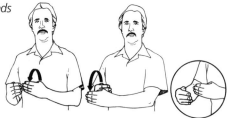

read **1.** To transfer information from computer storage into memory. **2.** To input information, as by a scanner. See sign for SCAN.

read error A system interrupt that is triggered when the computer is unable to access a particular area of data.

■ **read** Move the fingertips of the right *V hand* down across the palm of the left *open hand* with a double movement.

■ **wrong** Bring the middle fingers of the right *Y hand*, palm in, back against the chin with a deliberate movement.

README See sign for README FILE.

readme file or **README** A small text file that comes with many software packages and contains up-to-date information not included in the official documentation.

■ **read** Move the fingertips of the right *V hand* down across the palm of the left *open hand* with a double movement.

■ **me** Point the extended right index finger to the center of the chest.

■ **file** Slide the little-finger side of the right *B hand*, palm angled up, between the fingers of the left *5 hand*, palm facing in, first between the index and middle fingers and then between the middle and ring fingers.

read-only files See sign for PROTECTED FILES.

read-only memory See sign for ROM.

real address See sign for ABSOLUTE ADDRESS.

real-time processing The processing of data by an operating system that responds to input immediately.

- **now** Bring both *Y hands,* palms facing up, downward in front of each side of the body.

- **time** Tap the bent index finger of the right *X hand*, palm down, with a double movement on the wrist of the downturned left hand.

- **process** Beginning with both *open hands* in front of the body, palms facing in, left fingers pointing right and right fingers pointing left, and the left hand closer to the chest than the right hand, move the left over the right hand and then the right over the left hand in an alternating movement.

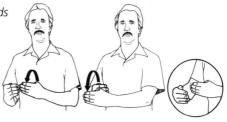

reboot See signs for WARM BOOT[1,2,3].

record (noun) A complete set of information in database management systems.

- **column** Move the right *modified C hand*, palm forward, from in front of the right shoulder downward.

- **row** Move the right *modified C hand*, palm forward, from in front of the chest outward to the right.

recover

recover **1.** To restore a deleted file. **2.** To continue program execution after a failure. Same sign used for **undelete, UnErase**.

- **recover** Beginning with the fingertips of both *curved hands* entwined in front of the chest, palms down, bend the wrists to raise the fingers upward, ending with the palms angled toward each other.

recursive[1] Of or being a procedure that can be called from within itself and used repeatedly to complete some task. Related forms: **recursion, recursively**.

- **call[1]** Slap the fingers of the right *open hand* on the back of the left *open hand*, both palms facing down, dragging the right fingers upward and closing them into an *A hand* in front of the right side of the chest.

- **itself** Bring the knuckles of the right *10 hand*, palm in, firmly against the side of the extended left index finger, palm forward and finger pointing up in front of the chest.

recursive[2] (alternate sign) Related forms: **recursion, recursively**.

- **recursion** Move the right *R hand*, palm forward, from in front of the right shoulder downward in a repeated circular movement.

redial To dial again, typically after getting a busy signal or no connection, through a dial-up modem.

- **call[2]** Bring the index finger of the right *X hand*, palm down, from the base off the fingertip of the extended left index finger held in front of the chest, palm right and finger pointing forward.

- **again** Bring the fingertips of the right *bent hand* against the palm of the left *open hand* held in front of the chest

redirect To send output or input to a device other than the default device, such as sending e-mail to a printer instead of to the display screen where it is usually sent by default. Related form: **redirection**.

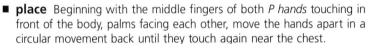

- **send** With a quick movement, flick the fingertips of the right *bent hand* forward across the back of the left *open hand*, both palms facing down, straightening the fingers as the right hand moves forward.

- **other** Beginning with the right *10 hand* in front of the chest, palm down, flip the hand over to the right, ending with palm up.

- **place** Beginning with the middle fingers of both *P hands* touching in front of the body, palms facing each other, move the hands apart in a circular movement back until they touch again near the chest.

redlining A method of marking edited text in a word processing document so that someone else can see what has been deleted, added, or changed.

- **edit** With the extended right index finger, palm forward, make small repeated crosses on the palm of the left *open hand*, palm in, in front of the chest.

- **red** Brush the extended right index finger downward on the lips.

reduced instruction set computer See sign for RISC.

reformat 1. To change the style of text in a document. 2. To convert a computer file for use by a different application.

- **form** Beginning with the fingertips of both *F hands* touching in front of the chest, palms facing forward, bring the hands away from each other to about shoulder width and then straight down a short distance.

---- [sign continues] -->

reformat

- **again** Beginning with the right *bent hand* beside the left *curved hand*, both palms up, bring the right hand up while turning it over, ending with the fingertips of the right hand touching the palm of the left hand.

---

refresh or **reload** To direct a Web browser to cause up-dated information to be sent to the display screen. Same sign used for **New**.

- **new** Slide the back of the right *curved hand*, palm up, across the palm of the upturned left *open hand*.

---

register A storage area in the computer's memory where data resides that is to be processed.

- **register** Touch the fingertips of the right *R hand*, palm down, first to the heel and then to the fingertips of the palm of the left *open hand*.

Registry The database used to store the Windows configuration on an individual computer; it is reloaded each time Windows is run. Settings in the Registry are determined by the hardware, which peripherals are attached, and which application programs are installed, as well as by recorded user preferences.

- **window** Beginning with the little-finger side of the right *B hand* on the index-finger side of the left *B hand*, both palms facing in and fingers pointing in opposite directions, move the right hand up and the left hand down simultaneously.

- **choose** Beginning with the bent thumb and index finger of the right *5 hand* touching the index finger of the left *V hand*, palms facing each other, pull the right hand upward while pinching the thumb and index finger together. Repeat from the middle finger of the left *V hand*.

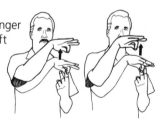

- **list**[1] Touch the little-finger side of the right *bent hand*, palm in, from the fingertips of the left *open hand* down the left forearm.

relational database A type of database that stores information in related tables that allow the user to access the information stored in one table, such as records of orders, through another table, such as customer names.

- **connect** Beginning with both *curved 5 hands* in front of each side of the body, palms facing each other, bring the hands together while touching the thumb and index fingertips of each hand and intersecting with each other.

- **file** Slide the little-finger side of the right *B hand,* palm angled up, between the fingers of the left *5 hand,* palm facing in, first between the index and middle fingers and then between the middle and ring fingers.

- Fingerspell: D-B

relative address A location in a computer's memory as specified by indicating its distance from another address, called the *base address.* Compare ABSOLUTE ADDRESS, ADDRESS.

- **relative** Beginning with both *R hands* in front of each side of the chest, palms facing down and fingers pointing forward, move the hands up and down with a double alternating movement.

- **address** Move both *A hands,* palms facing in, upward on each side of the chest with a double movement.

reload See sign for REFRESH.

REM Abbreviation of *Remark.* A program command that instructs the computer to ignore the rest of the line, thus allowing the programmer to place a comment or explanation in the program without concern that the computer will view it as a command.

- Fingerspell: R-E-M

Remark See sign for REM.

remote 1. Descriptive of communications between computers over telephone lines. 2. Descriptive of a computer or peripheral that is not in the immediate area of the host computer. Compare LOCAL.

- **far** Beginning with the palm sides of both *A hands* together in front of the chest, move the right hand forward in an arc.

remote access

remote access The ability of a computer to connect and interact with another computer or peripheral that is not in the immediate area.

- **far** Beginning with the palm sides of both *A hands* together in front of the chest, move the right hand forward in an arc.

- **connect** Beginning with left *curved 5 hand* in front of the chest, palm forward, and the right *curved 5 hand* somewhat forward, palm facing in, bring the left hand forward while touching the thumb and index fingertips of each hand and intersecting with each other.

removable disk See sign for REMOVABLE STORAGE.

removable storage or **removable disk** Any of a number of devices for storing data that are transportable outside the computer, such as CDs, floppy disks, or removable hard disks.

- **save** Tap the fingers of the right *V hand* with a double movement on the back of the left *S hand*, both palms facing in.

- **bring** Move both *open hands*, palms up, from in front of the right side of the body in large arcs to the left side of the body.

- **with** Beginning with both *A hands* in front of the chest, palms facing each other, bring the hands together.

- **you** Point the right extended index finger forward toward the referent.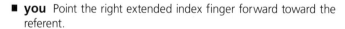

remove See sign for DELETE.

repeat key A program feature that provides for the ability of the last entry to be replicated by pressing a function key or a combination of keys.

- **again** Bring the fingertips of the right *bent hand* against the palm of the left *open hand* held in front of the chest.

- **copy** Move the fingers of the right *curved hand* from touching the palm of the left *open hand* while closing the right fingers and thumb forming a *flattened O hand*.

repetitive motion injury See sign for Carpal Tunnel Syndrome.

repetitive stress injury See sign for Carpal Tunnel Syndrome.

reply To respond to an e-mail message or a newsgroup posting. Same sign used for **report**.

- **reply** Beginning with the fingers of both *R hands* pointing up, right hand closer to the mouth than the left hand and the palms facing in opposite directions, move the hands forward and downward with a deliberate movement, ending with the palms facing down and fingers pointing forward.

report A document generated by a computer program that summarizes the outcome from data processing. See sign for REPLY.

reset See signs for WARM BOOT[1,2,3].

resident font, internal font, or **built-in font** The font or fonts built into a printer when it is manufactured.

- **finish** With both *5 hands* apart in front of the body, palms facing up, quickly turn the hands over toward each other, ending with the palms down and fingers pointing forward.

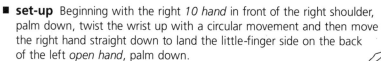

- **set-up** Beginning with the right *10 hand* in front of the right shoulder, palm down, twist the wrist up with a circular movement and then move the right hand straight down to land the little-finger side on the back of the left *open hand*, palm down.

- Fingerspell: F-O-N-T

resident program

resident program[1] or **supervisor program** A program that stays in a dedicated area of a computer's main memory at all times while the computer is on. Compare TRANSIENT.

- **finish** With both *5 hands* apart in front of the body, palms facing up, quickly turn the hands over toward each other, ending with the palms down and fingers pointing forward.

- **set-up** Beginning with the right *10 hand* in front of the right shoulder, palm down, twist the wrist up with a circular movement and then move the right hand straight down to land the little-finger side on the back of the left *open hand*, palm down.

- **program** Move the middle finger of the right *P hand*, palm left, from the fingertips to the base of the left *open hand*, palm right and fingers pointing up. Repeat the movement on the back side of the left hand.

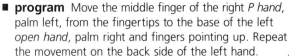

---

resident program[2] or **supervisor program** (alternate sign)

- **supervise** With the little-finger side of the right *K hand* on the thumb side of the left *K hand*, palms facing in opposite directions, move the hands in a flat circle in front of the body.

- **program** Move the middle finger of the right *P hand*, palm left, from the fingertips to the base of the left *open hand*, palm right and fingers pointing up. Repeat the movement on the back side of the left hand.

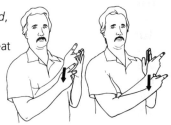

---

resolution The relative fineness or clarity of a picture image or text as measured in *pixels* for a display screen or expressed as *dpi (dots per inch)* when produced by a scanner or printer.

- **picture** Move the right *C hand*, palm forward, from near the right side of the face downward, ending with the index-finger side of the right *C hand* against the palm of the left *open hand* held in front of the chest, palm right.

---- [sign continues] -->

■ **quality** Shake the right *Q hand*, palm down and fingers pointing down, in front of the chest.

resource Anything available for use by a computer, such as memory, a monitor, a printer, etc.

■ **resource** Beginning with the right *R hand* in front of the body, palm left, move the hand in a double arc to the right.

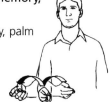

restore To copy files from an archive or set of backup disks to their original locations on the hard disk. Compare BACK UP.

■ **import** Beginning with both *V hands*, palms facing each other and fingers pointing up, near the right shoulder, bring the hands down to the left while bending the extended fingers.

■ **save** Tap the fingers of the right *V hand* with a double movement on the back of the left *S hand*, both palms facing in.

retrieve See sign for OPEN.

Return key See sign for ENTER KEY.

reverse video A video display screen that reverses the usual foreground and background colors. On a monochrome display, as when running the DOS operating system, reverse video has dark characters on a light background, which is the inverse of the normal.

■ **video** With the thumb of the right *5 hand*, palm forward, against the palm of the left *open hand*, palm right and fingers pointing up, wiggle the right fingers.

■ **screen** Beginning with both extended index fingers side by side in front of the chest, palms facing down and fingers pointing forward, bring the hands apart to in front of each shoulder, then straight down, and finally back together again in front of the lower chest.

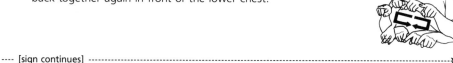

---- [sign continues] -->

reverse video

- **color** Wiggle the fingers of the right *5 hand* in front of the mouth, fingers pointing up and palm facing in.

- **reverse** Beginning with both *V hands* in front of the chest, right palm in and fingers pointing left, and left palm out and fingers pointing right, twist the hands in opposite directions to turn the palms the opposite way.

---

rich text format See sign for RTF.

---

right-click On a two-button mouse, such as one typically used for a PC rather than a Mac, to press on the mouse's right button rather than the left button, which is the one normally used.

- **mouse**[1] Move the right *modified C hand*, palm forward, around in front of the right side of the body.

- **right**[1] Move the right extended index finger, palm forward and finger pointing right, to the right a short distance in front of the right side of the body.

- **click** Beginning with the right index finger pointing forward in front of the chest, bend the finger deliberately downward.

---

right-justify To align (text) on the right column or margin, with the text more or less ragged on the left.

- **right**[2] Move the right *R hand*, palm down, from in front of the right side of the chest to the right.

---- [sign continues] --→

- **side**[2] Move the right *open hand*, palm left and fingers pointing forward, downward in front the right side of the body.

RISC Acronym for *reduced instruction set computer*. A computer that runs very fast because the microprocessor is limited to using a relatively small number of instructions.

- Fingerspell: R-I-S-C

ROM Acronym for *read-only memory*. Memory built into a computer's operating system that can be accessed but cannot be altered.

- Fingerspell: R-O-M

root directory The primary directory of a hierarchical file structure that holds the first tier of named directories as well as the operating system command and system configuration files. Same sign used for **default directory**.

- **start** Beginning with the extended right index finger, palm down, inserted between the index and middle fingers of the left *open hand*, palm right and fingers pointing forward, twist the right hand back, ending with palm in.

- **directory** Move the fingertips of the right *D hand*, palm down, across the palm of the left *open hand* with a double circular movement.

routine or **modules** A group of computer commands designed to perform a particular task.

- **routine** Move the fingers of the right *R hand*, palm in and fingers pointing left, from the palm side of the left *open hand* held in front of the body, palm in, in an arc over to the back side of the left hand.

routing The assignment of a path for the delivery of a message, as over the Internet. See sign for PATH.

row 1. The horizontal arrangement of data in a spreadsheet or table. 2. A line of text in a word-processing document or a line of text across a display screen.

- **row** Move the right *modified C hand,* palm forward, from in front of the chest outward to the right.

RTF Initialism for *rich text format.* A file format that is readable by most major word processors consisting of ASCII text with hidden instructions that describe the document's formatting.

- Fingerspell: R-T-F

run See sign for EXECUTE.

runtime or **run-time** 1. The period required for a computer to perform a particular task, such as a mail merge. 2. Taking place during the running or execution of a program.

- **run** Brush the palm of the right *open hand* upward with a double movement on the palm of the left *open hand* held in front of the chest.

- **time** Tap the bent index finger of the right *X hand*, palm down, with a double movement on the wrist of the downturned left hand.

---

satellite An earth-orbiting device capable of relaying communications signals over long distances.

- **satellite** Beginning with the right *curved 5 hand,* palm down and fingers pointing down, near the extended left index finger held in front of the chest, palm in and finger pointing up, move the right hand to in front of the left side of the chest and then back to in front of the right shoulder.

---

save[1]**, store,** or **storage** **1.** To store data in permanent form, usually on a disk. **2. Save** The command that saves data. Same sign used for **capture**.

- **save** Tap the fingers of the right *V hand,* palm up, with a double movement on the little-finger side of the left *S hand* held in front of the chest, palm in.

---

save[2]**, store,** or **storage** (alternate sign used when referring to long-term storage)

- **store** Insert the fingertips of the right *flattened O hand,* palm left, into the center of the thumb side of the left *O hand,* palm angled forward.

---

scale To change the size of a graphics file by a specified quantity to make it fit a specified boundary. Related form: **scalable, scaling**.

- **measure** Beginning with the thumbs of both *Y hands* touching in front of the chest, palms down, bring the hands apart to each side.

- **big** Hold both *open hands* apart in front of each side of the chest, palms facing each other.

---- [sign continues] -->

■ **small** Hold both *open hands* near each other in front of the chest, palms facing each other.

scan To read text, images, or bar codes into a computer by using a device called a scanner. Same sign used for **read**.

■ **read** With a double movement, move the fingertips of the right *V hand* down across the palm of the left *open hand*.

scanner or **optical scanner** A device that can electronically capture printed documents, pictures, or even handwriting for use by a computer.

■ **scan** Move the bent index finger of the right *X hand*, palm left, back and forth with a repeated movement under the palm of the left *open hand*, palm down.

schedule A list of events in the order in which they should occur. See sign for GRAPH.

scheduler A program, often part of an electronic mail system, used to schedule meetings according to convenient times found on the users' shared calendars.

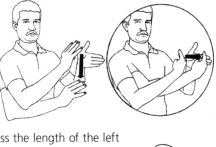

■ **schedule** Beginning with the left *open hand* held in front of the left shoulder, palm right and fingers pointing forward, bring the fingers of the right *4 hand*, palm left, down the heel of the left hand, and then drag the back of the right fingers across the length of the left palm from the heel to the fingertips.

■ **person marker** Move both *open hands*, palms facing each other, downward along the sides of the body.

schema The structure of a database.

- Fingerspell: D-B

- **structure** Beginning with the left *S hand* on the back of the right *S hand,* both palms facing down, move the right hand in a forward and upward arc to reverse positions. Repeat as the hands move upward in front of the chest.

Scrapbook A desk accessory on the Macintosh computer that stores frequently used graphics images or text for pasting into documents. See sign for CLIPBOARD.

screen See sign for DISPLAY SCREEN.

screen blanker See signs for SCREEN SAVER[1,2].

screen capture or **screen dump** The act of copying whatever is currently displayed on the display screen to a file or printer.

- **screen** Beginning with both extended index fingers side by side in front of the chest, palms facing down and fingers pointing forward, bring the hands apart to in front of each shoulder, then straight down, and finally back together again in front of the lower chest.

- **copy**[2] Move the fingers of the right *curved hand* from touching the extended index finger of the left *one hand* while closing the right fingers and thumb forming a *flattened O hand.*

screen dump See sign for SCREEN CAPTURE.

screen saver[1] or **screen blanker** A utility or program that period- ically blanks out the screen and replaces it with darkness or a graphic image to prevent the same image from "burning in" the screen permanently.

- **screen** Beginning with both extended index fingers side by side in front of the chest, palms facing down and fingers pointing forward, bring the hands apart to in front of each shoulder, then straight down, and finally back together again in front of the lower chest.

- **save** Tap the fingers of the right *V hand* with a double movement on the back of the left *S hand,* both palms facing in.

screen saver

screen saver[2] or screen blanker (alternate sign)

■ **screen** Beginning with both extended index fingers side by side in front of the chest, palms facing down and fingers pointing forward, bring the hands apart to in front of each shoulder, then straight down, and finally back together again in front of the lower chest.

■ **protect** With the wrists of both *S hands* crossed in front of the chest, palms facing in opposite directions, move the hands forward with a short double movement.

---

scroll To move through copy line by line on a computer display screen. Related form: **scrolling**.

■ **scroll** Beginning with the little finger of the right *4 hand* on the index finger of the left *4 hand*, both palms facing in and fingers pointing in opposite directions in front of the chest, move the hands upward in front of the chest with a double movement.

---

scroll bar A vertical or horizontal strip that appears on the right or bottom side of a window and lets you use a mouse to scroll the image up and down or left and right.

■ **scroll** Beginning with the little finger of the right *4 hand* on the index finger of the left *4 hand*, both palms facing in and fingers pointing in opposite directions in front of the chest, move the hands upward in front of the chest with a double movement.

■ **bar** Move the fingers of the right *G hand*, palm forward, from left to right in front of the chest.

SCSI (pronounced *skuzz-ee*) Acronym for *Small Computer System Interface*. A controller that transfers data at high speeds and supports as many as seven peripherals, including hard drives, through a single expansion slot.

■ Fingerspell: S-C-S-I

---

search A feature in some programs that scans to locate a word or phrase (or even a particular special character) in text files, records, or on the Internet. Same sign used for **browse**. Compare FIND.

■ **search** Move the right *C hand*, palm left, with a double circular movement in front of the face.

search and replace See sign for FIND AND REPLACE.

search engine or **Web catalog** Any one of a variety of Web browser software programs that give you the ability to search for Internet resources.

- **search** Move the right *C hand*, palm left, with a double circular movement in front of the face.

- **machine** With the fingers of both *curved 5 hands* loosely meshed together, palms facing in, move the hands up and down in front of the chest with a repeated movement.

search item or **search string** The word or words that a computer is directed to look for when searching either in its memory or online on the Internet.

- **search** Move the right *C hand*, palm left, with a double circular movement in front of the face.

- **word** Touch the extended fingers of the right *G hand*, palm left, against the extended left index finger pointing up in front of the chest, palm right.

search string See sign for SEARCH ITEM.

secondary storage See signs for MASS STORAGE[1,2].

sector The smallest unit of disk storage that can be accessed; part of one of the concentric tracks into which a computer disk is divided.

- **disk** Move the fingertips of the right *D hand*, palm facing down and index finger pointing forward, in a double circle on the upturned left *open hand*.

- **parts** Slide the little-finger side of the right *open hand*, palm left, with a double movement across the palm of the left *open hand*, palm up, moving to a different section of the left hand each time.

seek time See sign for ACCESS TIME.

segment In a personal computer, a 64K portion of memory. See sign for ALLOCATE[1].

select[1] See sign for BLOCK.

select[2] To choose from the alternatives offered by clicking on one of them. See sign for OPTIONS.

Send A command used to forward electronic mail to the recipient.

- **send** With a quick movement, flick the fingertips of the right *bent hand* forward across the back of the left *open hand*, both palms facing down, straightening the fingers as the right hand moves forward.

sequential or **serial** Descriptive of data, files, etc., that are arranged in an ordered manner. Same sign used for **sort, order**.

- **plan** Move both *open hands* from in front of the left side of the body, palms facing each other and fingers pointing forward, in a long smooth movement to in front of the right side of the body.

sequential access The necessity, in some systems or on some media, to search files serially from the beginning to find any given record. Compare DIRECT ACCESS.

- **list**[2] Move the right *bent hand*, palm left, downward in a series of steps in front of the right side of the body.

- **search** Move the right *C hand*, palm left, with a double circular movement in front of the face.

sequential processing The processing of files that are ordered numerically or alphabetically by key. Compare RANDOM PROCESSING.

- **list**[2] Move the right *bent hand*, palm left, downward in a series of steps in front of the right side of the body.

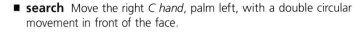

---- [sign continues] --→

- **process** Beginning with both *open hands* in front of the body, palms facing in, left fingers pointing right and right fingers pointing left, and the left hand closer to the chest than the right hand, move the left over the right hand and then the right over the left hand in an alternating movement.

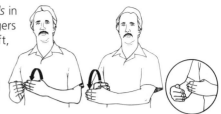

serial See sign for SEQUENTIAL.

serial interface[1] A channel that transmits data one bit after another.

- **one** Hold the extended index finger of the right *one hand*, palm back, in front of the right shoulder.

- **interface** Beginning with both *5 hands* in front of each side of the chest, fingers angled toward each other, push the hands toward each other, causing the fingers to mesh.

serial interface[2] or **serial port** A port that manages communication between the computer and a device, such as a printer or modem, and other computers one bit at a time.

- **one** Hold the extended index finger of the right *one hand*, palm back, in front of the right shoulder.

- **port** Touch the fingertips of the right *G hand*, palm left, against the palm of the left *open hand*, palm right and fingers pointing up.

serial port See sign for SERIAL INTERFACE[2].

server, printer server, or **slave** A high-capacity computer with resources such as a hard disk and printer that are available to other terminals in a computer network.

- **serve** Beginning with both *open hands* in front of each side of the body, palms facing up and right hand closer to the body than the left, move the hands forward and back with an alternating movement.

---- [sign continues] ---➤

server

- **person marker** Move both *open hands*, palms facing each other, downward along the sides of the body.

service provider See signs for ONLINE SERVICE[1,2].

setup See sign for INITIALIZE[1].

SGML Initialism for *Standard Generalized Markup Language.* A language that enables the user to create an appropriate markup scheme for tagging the elements of an electronic document according to the types of content in the elements. This allows the use of external style sheets for applying more than one way of formatting and presenting the same information.

- Fingerspell: S-G-M-L

shared resources Devices, peripherals, programs, etc., that serve two or more computers or terminals.

- **share** Move the little-finger side of the right *open hand*, palm in, back and forth with a double movement at the base of the index finger of the left *open hand*, palm in.

- **equipment** Move the right *E hand*, palm up, from in front of the middle of the body to the right in a double arc.

shareware[1] or **freeware** Copyrighted software that can be freely copied but not sold. The developers of shareware programs often distribute them with the understanding that those who make continued use of a program will pay a small fee suggested by the developer.

- **free** Beginning with both *S hands* crossed at the wrists in front of the chest, palms facing in opposite directions, twist the wrists and move the hands apart, ending with the hands in front of each shoulder, palms facing forward.
- Fingerspell: W-A-R-E

shareware[2] or **freeware** (alternate sign)

- **share** Move the little-finger side of the right *open hand,* palm in, back and forth with a double movement at the base of the index finger of the left *open hand,* palm in.
- Fingerspell: W-A-R-E

sheet feeder See sign for PAPER FEED.

shell A utility program designed to simplify a program or operating system that is considered difficult to use.

- Fingerspell: S-H-E-L-L

Shift key A keyboard key that in combination with other keys causes them to become uppercase, or capital, letters. On the numbers row, the Shift key allows the keying of additional symbols.

- **capital** Hold the right *modified C hand,* palm forward, in front of the right shoulder.

- **key** Push the extended thumb of the right *10 hand* downward a short distance in front of the right side of the body.

shortcut An icon that connects to a small special file that provides fast access to a program. See sign for ACRONYM.

shortcut key See signs for MACRO[1,2].

shut down To turn off the power source to the computer. See sign for OFF-LINE.

sign on See sign for LOG IN.

sign out See sign for LOG OUT.

Silicon Valley A place in northern California that is known for making semiconductors, microprocessors, and other computer electronic circuitry.

- Fingerspell: S-I-L-I-C-O-N
- **valley** Beginning with both *B hands* in front of each side of the head, palms facing down and fingers pointing forward, move the hands downward toward each other, ending with the index-finger sides of both hands touching in front of the body.

Simple Mail Transfer Protocol

Simple Mail Transfer Protocol See sign for SMTP.

simple sequence A programming language where the instructions to the computer are executed in the order in which they appear.

- **simple** Beginning with both *F hands* in front of the body, the right hand higher than the left and palms facing each other, bring the right hand down, striking the fingertips of the left hand as it passes.

- **list**[2] Move the right *bent hand*, palm left, downward in a series of steps in front of the right side of the body.

simulation[1] A representation or imitation on a computer of an object or situation; used for instruction.

- **fake** Beginning with the index finger of the right *4 hand* touching the right side of the forehead, move the hand forward in several short movements.

- **teach** Move both *flattened O hands*, palms facing each other, forward with a short double movement in front of each side of the head.

simulation[2] (alternate sign)

- **do** Move both *C hands*, palms facing down, from side to side with a repeated movement in front of the body.

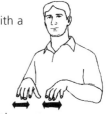

- **same** Beginning with both index fingers pointing forward in front of each side of the body, palms facing down, bring the hands together, ending with the index fingers side by side in front of the body.

simulation[3] A computer game that reflects aspects of the real world.

■ **computer**[1] Move the thumb side of the right *C hand,* palm left, from touching the lower part of the extended left arm upward to touch the upper arm.

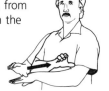

■ **game** Bring the knuckles of both *10 hands*, palms facing in, against each other with a double movement in front of the chest.

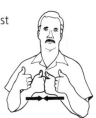

simultaneous See signs for CONCURRENT[1,2].

single-user Refers to software that is licensed for use by one person only.

■ **one** Hold the extended index finger of the right *one hand*, palm back, in front of the right shoulder.

■ **person** Move both *P hands*, palms facing each other, downward along the sides of the body.

■ **use** Beginning with the heel of the right *U hand* on the back of the left *S hand*, move the right hand in a small upward circle.

skip[1] To ignore one or more instructions in a sequence of instructions.

■ **skip**[1] Touch the fingertip of the right *X hand* first to the index finger and then the ring finger of the left *5 hand*, palm in.

skip

skip[2] (alternate sign)

- **skip[2]** Tap the palm side of the right bent *V hand*, palm forward, first on the index finger and then the middle finger of the left *5 hand* held in front of the chest, palm in.

---

slack time See sign for FLOAT.

---

slash See sign for FORWARD SLASH.

---

slave See sign for SERVER.

---

slice A special type of chip architecture that permits the cascading of devices to increase word bit size.

- **slice** Bring the palm side of the right *open hand*, palm left and fingers pointing forward, from in front of the chest straight down near the thumb side of the left *S hand* held in front of the body, palm down.

---

slide A photographic transparency on film arranged for projection.

- **slide** Beginning with both *H hands* in front of the chest, palms facing in, left fingers pointing right, and right fingers pointing left, move the right fingers to the left across the back of the left fingers with a double movement.

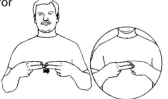

---

slider The bar, usually on the side or bottom of a display on the screen, that permits the user to shift the contents horizontally or vertically for better viewing.

- **slider** Move the extended right index finger from the base to the fingertip of the left extended index finger held in front of the chest, palm in and finger pointing right.

---

slot A long, thin opening in a computer frame, or motherboard, into which an expansion card is plugged.

- Fingerspell: S-L-O-T

Small Computer System Interface See sign for SCSI.

---

smart card A credit card having a built-in computer.

- **smart** Bring the bent middle finger of the right *5 hand* from touching the forehead, palm in, forward while turning the palm forward.

---- [sign continues] -->

- **card** Beginning with the fingertips of both *L hands* touching in front of the chest, palms facing forward, bring the hands apart to in front of each shoulder and then pinch each thumb and index finger together.

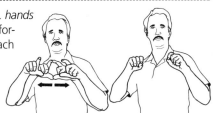

smart media card A small card having a built-in computer on which digital photographic images are stored.

- **smart** Bring the bent middle finger of the right *5 hand* from touching the forehead, palm in, forward while turning the palm forward.

- **picture** Move the right *C hand*, palm forward, from near the right side of the face downward, ending with the index-finger side of the right *C hand* against the palm of the left *open hand* held in front of the chest, palm right.

- **card** Beginning with the fingertips of both *L hands* touching in front of the chest, palms facing forward, bring the hands apart to in front of each shoulder and then pinch each thumb and index finger together.

smart terminal See sign for INTELLIGENT TERMINAL.

SMTP Initialism for *Simple Mail Transfer Protocol*. The basic way text messages are exchanged on the Internet.

- Fingerspell: S-M-T-P

snail mail A derisive term used by e-mail users to describe the postal service.

- **slow** Pull the fingers of the right *5 hand* from the fingers to the wrist of the left *open hand*, both palms down.

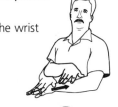

- **letter** Touch the extended thumb of the right *10 hand* to the lips, palm in, and then move the thumb downward to touch the thumb of the left *10 hand* held in front of the chest, palm in.

- Fingerspell: P-O

soft copy A temporary form of output such as a monitor display.

- **soft** Beginning with both *curved 5 hands* in front of each side of the chest, palms up, bring the hands down with a double movement while closing the fingers to the thumbs each time.

- **copy**[1] Move the fingers of the right *curved hand* from touching the palm of the left *open hand* while closing the right fingers and thumb, forming a *flattened O hand*.

soft return In word processing, an automatic forced end to a line of text within a paragraph that moves overflow text to the next line. A soft return is temporary, moving to a different place to accommodate additions or deletions to the line of text.

- **soft** Beginning with both *curved 5 hands* in front of each side of the chest, palms up, bring the hands down with a double movement while closing the fingers to the thumbs each time.

- **return** Beginning with the right *R hand*, palm down and fingers pointing forward, in front of the right side of the chest, twist the hand over, ending with the palm facing up.

software[1] System, utility, or application programs expressed in a computer-readable language.

- Fingerspell: S-W

software[2] (alternate sign)

- **soft** Beginning with both *curved 5 hands* in front of each side of the chest, palms up, bring the hands down with a double movement while closing the fingers to the thumbs each time.
- Fingerspell: W-A-R-E

software package A computer program in complete and ready-to-run form, including all necessary programs and documentation.

- Fingerspell: S-W

---- [sign continues] -->

■ **box** Beginning with both *open hands* in front of each side of the chest, palms facing each other and fingers pointing forward, move the hands deliberately in opposite directions, ending with the left hand near the chest and the right hand several inches forward of the left hand, both palms facing in.

---

software piracy See sign for PIRACY.

---

software tools See sign for UTILITY.

---

sort To place data or files in a predetermined order such as alphabetical, by date, by number, etc. See sign for SEQUENTIAL.

---

sound board or **sound card** An adapter that adds digital sound and music capabilities to a computer.

■ **hear** Touch the right ear with the extended right index finger.

■ **card** Beginning with the fingertips of both *L hands* touching in front of the chest, palms facing forward, bring the hands apart to in front of each shoulder and then pinch each thumb and index finger together.

---

sound card See sign for SOUND BOARD.

---

source When data is moved from one place to another, the original place from which the data is moved is called the *source*. Compare DESTINATION. See sign for ACTIVATE.

---

source code[1] The typed program instructions that programmers write before the program has been interpreted into machine instructions that the computer can execute.

■ **start** Beginning with the extended right index finger, palm down, inserted between the index and middle fingers of the left *open hand*, palm right and fingers pointing forward, twist the right hand back, ending with palm in.

■ Fingerspell: C-O-D-E

source code

source code[2] (alternate sign)

- **start** Beginning with the extended right index finger, palm down, inserted between the index and middle fingers of the left *open hand*, palm right and fingers pointing forward, twist the right hand back, ending with palm in.

- **program** Move the middle finger of the right *P hand*, palm left, from the fingertips to the base of the left *open hand*, palm right and fingers pointing up. Repeat the movement on the back side of the left hand.

---

space The character or blank produced by pressing the spacebar. See sign for SPACING.

---

spacebar The long, narrow key at the bottom of the keyboard that produces a blank space when pressed.

- **empty** Move the bent middle fingertip of the right *5 hand* across the back of the left *open hand* from the wrist to off the fingertips, both palms facing down.
- Fingerspell: B-A-R

---

spacing The horizontal space between rows of characters in a document. Same sign used for **space**.

- **empty** Move the bent middle fingertip of the right *5 hand* across the back of the left *open hand* from the wrist to off the fingertips, both palms facing down.

- **row** Move the right *modified C hand*, palm forward, from in front of the chest outward to the right.

---

spam (Sometimes capitalized.) Unwanted, and often annoying, e-mail, usually advertising some product or scheme and sent out to large numbers of recipients.

- Fingerspell: S-P-A-M

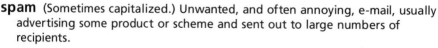

speech recognition See sign for VOICE RECOGNITION.

speech synthesis Artificial human speech created by a computer through the use of recorded sounds from digital data.

- **fake** Beginning with the index finger of the right *4 hand* touching the right side of the forehead, move the hand forward in several short movements.

- **speech** Move the bent fingers of the right *V hand,* palm in, in a small repeated circle in front of the mouth.

speed The access time of a computer's microprocessor as measured in megahertz or gigahertz.

- **how** Beginning with the knuckles of both *curved hands* touching in front of the chest, palms facing down, twist the hands upward and forward, ending with the fingers together pointing up and the palm facing up.

- **fast** Beginning with the extended index fingers of both *one hands* pointing forward in front of the chest, pull the hands back toward the chest while changing to *S hands.*

spell-check program See sign for DICTIONARY PROGRAM.

spike See sign for SURGE.

spooler A device that is used to store computer output so it can be sent to the printer in sequential order or printed at a later time. Related forms: **spool, spooling**.

- **spool** Move the extended right index finger, palm in and finger pointing left, in a forward circle with a repeated movement near the index-finger side of the left *S hand* held in front of the chest, palm down.

spreadsheet 1. A document arranged in rows and columns where data, especially numerical data, can be entered and manipulated for reporting. 2. Referring to a software program designed to handle such documents.

- **spread** Beginning with the fingers of both *flattened O hands* together in front of the chest, palms facing down, move the hands forward and apart while opening into *5 hands.*

---- [sign continues] --->

spreadsheet

- **chart** Bring the right *4 hand* from in front of the left shoulder, palm in and fingers pointing left, to the right in front of the chest.

SRAM See sign for STATIC MEMORY.

---

stacking order Refers to a data structure that programmers use to store and remove information in the order in which it was most recently called.

- **stack** With an alternating movement, bring each *open hand* upward over the other hand in a small arc as the hands raise in front of the chest, both palms facing down and fingers angled in opposite directions.

- **plan** Move both *open hands* from in front of the left side of the body, palms facing each other and fingers pointing forward, in a long smooth movement to in front of the right side of the body.

---

stand-alone

- **stand** Move the fingertips of the right *V hand*, palm in and fingers pointing down, on the palm of the left *open hand* held in front of the body, palm up.

- **alone** Move the right extended index finger, palm back and finger pointing up, in a small circle in front of the right shoulder.

---

standard A guide established to measure the performance of any computer system function.

- **standard** Move both *Y hands* from side to side in front of the body, palms facing down.

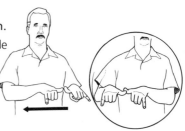

Standard Generalized Markup Language See sign for SGML.

start See sign for ACTIVATE.

state or **status** Refers to the condition of devices used to represent binary digits. The state of a switch describes whether it is off or on.

- **situation** Move the right *S hand* in a circle around the extended left index finger, palm facing right in front of the chest, by twisting the right wrist.

statement See sign for MESSAGE.

static memory or **SRAM** Computer memory that is retained when the power is off such as memory on a hard disk, floppy disk, CD, etc. Compare DYNAMIC MEMORY.

- **save** Tap the fingers of the right *V hand* with a double movement on the back of the left *S hand*, both palms facing in.

- **memory** Beginning with the fingertips of the right *curved hand* touching the right side of the forehead, palm down, bring the hand forward and down while closing the fingers into an *S hand*, palm in.

status See sign for STATE.

storage See signs for SAVE[1,2].

storage map See sign for MAP.

store See signs for SAVE[1,2]. Related form: **storage**.

streaming A media format that begins playing back or displaying content as soon as the data starts coming from the server, as opposed to the formats that require the entire file to download before beginning to play. Related form: **stream**.

- **stream** Beginning with both *B hands* in front of the right side of the chest, right palm up and left palm down, move the hands downward to the left with a double movement.

structure chart or **hierarchy chart** The design tool that shows the top- down design of a program.

- **chart** Bring the right *4 hand* from in front of the left shoulder, palm in and fingers pointing left, to the right in front of the chest.

---- [sign continues] -->

structure chart

- **node** Beginning with the index-finger sides of both *B hands* touching in front of the chest, palms facing in and fingers pointing down, move the hands down and apart while opening the fingers to *5 hands*.

structured programming A method of organizing and writing programs in small modules to make them easier to read and understand.

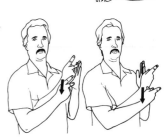

- **structure** Beginning with the left *S hand* on the back of the right *S hand*, both palms down, move the right hand in a forward and upward arc to reverse positions. Repeat as the hands move upward in front of the chest.

- **program** Move the middle finger of the right *P hand*, palm left, from the fingertips to the base of the left *open hand*, palm right and fingers pointing up. Repeat the movement on the back side of the left hand.

style Text formatting and character attributes combined to refer to the way text looks.

- Fingerspell: S-T-Y-L-E

style sheet A formatting template that is created in some programs to establish a master document with basic specifications.

- Fingerspell: S-T-Y-L-E
- **list**[1] Touch the little-finger side of the right *bent hand*, palm in, from the fingertips of the left *open hand* down the left forearm.

subdirectory or **folder** A directory created in another directory containing either files or other subdirectories.

- **under** Move the right *10 hand*, palm left, from in front of the chest downward and forward under the left *open hand* held in front of the chest, palm down and fingers pointing right.

---- [sign continues] --->

- **directory** Move the fingertips of the right *D hand*, palm down, across the palm of the left *open hand* with a double upward movement.

subordinate module In a structure chart, a module one level down from the superordinate module, to which control may be temporarily transferred.

- **under** Move the right *10 hand*, palm left, from in front of the chest downward and forward under the left *open hand* held in front of the chest, palm down and fingers pointing right.

- **groups** Beginning with both *C hands* in front of the right side of the chest, palms facing each other, bring the hands away from each other in outward arcs while turning the palms in, ending with the little fingers near each other. Repeat in front of the left side of the chest.

subroutine 1. A part of a computer program that can be used in a routine. 2. See sign for ROUTINE.

- **subroutine** Beginning with the index-finger side of the right *S hand* near the heel of the left *open hand*, palm right and fingers pointing up, move the right hand up the left palm while changing into an *R hand* and then down the back of the left hand.

subschema An outline of the fields that a user will be able to use in a database.

- Fingerspell: S-U-B

- **field** Move the fingertips of the right *F hand*, palm down, forward along the length of the index finger of the left *B hand*, palm right, from the base to the tip.

- **list**[1] Touch the little-finger side of the right *bent hand*, palm in, from the fingertips of the left *open hand* down the left forearm.

summary A condensed version of a document or compilation. See sign for ACRONYM.

supervisor program See signs for RESIDENT PROGRAM[1,2].

support Maintenance required to keep a computer system running.

■ **support** Push the knuckles of the right *S hand,* palm in, upward under the little-finger side of the left *S hand,* palm in, pushing the left hand upward a short distance in front of the chest.

support services or **customer support** Ongoing help available to the user from hardware or software manufacturers or vendors, sometimes via a toll-free telephone number or the Internet.

■ **help** With the little-finger side of the right *A hand* in the palm of the left *open hand,* move both hands upward in front of the chest.

■ **serve** Beginning with both *open hands* in front of each side of the body, palms facing up and right hand closer to the body than the left, move the hands forward and back with an alternating movement.

surf or **surf the Net** To explore the Internet, especially casually or recreationally, looking for interesting sites. Related form: **surfer.**

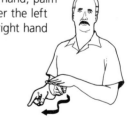

■ **search** Move the right *C hand,* palm left, with a double circular movement in front of the face.

■ **sneak** With the right index finger extended, move the right hand, palm down and finger pointing forward, in a wavy movement under the left *open hand,* sliding the left palm up the right forearm as the right hand moves forward.

surf the Net See sign for SURF.

surge or **spike** A sudden increase in electric current delivered through a power line that may damage a computer or its memory. Compare POWER SURGE.

- **electric** Tap the knuckles of the index fingers of both *X hands* together, palms facing in, with a double movement.

- **shock** Beginning with both *S hands* in front of each side of the body, palms facing down, move the hands forward and back with an alternating double movement.

surge protector An inexpensive electrical device that prevents high-voltage surges from reaching a computer and damaging its circuitry.

- **electric** Tap the knuckles of the index fingers of both *X hands* together, palms facing in, with a double movement.

- **shock** Beginning with both *S hands* in front of each side of the body, palms facing down, move the hands forward and back with an alternating double movement.

- **protect** With the wrists of both *S hands* crossed in front of the chest, palms facing in opposite directions, move the hands forward with a short double movement.

- **person marker** Move both *open hands*, palms facing each other, downward along the sides of the body.

swap file A dedicated section of a hard drive having virtual memory used to temporarily hold data when RAM is full, allowing the computer to call up more programs and data at one time than would be possible with RAM alone.

- **exchange** Beginning with both *modified X hands* in front of the body, right hand somewhat forward of the left hand, move the right hand back toward the body in an upward arc while moving the left hand forward with a downward arc.

- **file** Slide the little-finger side of the right *B hand*, palm angled up, between the fingers of the left *B hand*, palm facing in, first between the index and middle fingers and then between the middle and ring fingers.

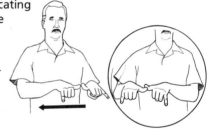

symbol Any of the characters available from the computer keyboard or from a chart of characters that one can click on.

- **symbol** With the index-finger side of the right *S hand*, palm forward, against the palm of the left *open hand* held in front of the chest, palm right and fingers pointing up, move both hands forward a short distance.

synchronous Of two computers, communicating at a specific pace with each other. Compare ASYNCHRONOUS.

- **standard** Move both *Y hands* from side to side in front of the body, palms facing down.

- **communication** Move both *C hands*, palms facing each other, forward and back from the mouth with an alternating movement.

syntax The rules governing the structure of commands, statements, or instructions that are given to a computer.

- **grammar** Beginning with the fingers of both *G hands* touching in front of the chest, palms facing each other, bring the hands apart with a wavy movement to in front of each side of the body.

syntax error A mistake in using the rules of language, such as typing a command incorrectly, that is detected by a language translator.

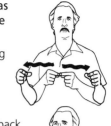

- **grammar** Beginning with the fingers of both *G hands* touching in front of the chest, palms facing each other, bring the hands apart with a wavy movement to in front of each side of the body.

- **wrong** Bring the middle fingers of the right *Y hand*, palm in, back against the chin with a deliberate movement.

---

system The whole computer, including the CPU, the peripherals, and the program that controls it.

- **system** Beginning with the index-finger sides of both *S hands* touching in front of the chest, palms down, move the hands apart to in front of each shoulder, and then down a short distance.

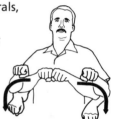

---

system analysis A part of systems development, especially in or for a business, in which the developers determine what the new system should accomplish and design it accordingly.

- **system** Beginning with the index-finger sides of both *S hands* touching in front of the chest, palms down, move the hands outward to in front of each shoulder and then straight down a short distance.

- **analyze** With both *V hands* pointing toward each other in front of the chest, palms down, move the fingers down and apart with a double movement, bending the fingers each time.

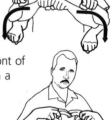

---

system backup See signs for FULL BACKUP[1,2].

system disk or **system software** All of the software used to operate and maintain a computer system.

- **system** Beginning with the index-finger sides of both *S hands* touching in front of the chest, palms down, move the hands outward to in front of each shoulder and then straight down a short distance.

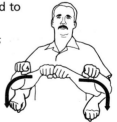

---- [sign continues] --->

system disk

■ **disk** Move the fingertips of the right *D hand,* palm facing down and index finger pointing forward, in a double circle on the upturned left *open hand.*

system resources All of the elements and devices available for use by a particular computer, such as type of CPU, memory, peripherals, etc.

■ **system** Beginning with the index-finger sides of both *S hands* touching in front of the chest, palms down, move the hands outward to in front of each shoulder and then straight down a short distance.

■ **resource** Beginning with the right *R hand* in front of the body, palm left, move the hand in a double arc to the right.

system software See sign for SYSTEM DISK.

tab A unit of specific space created by pressing the Tab key.

- Fingerspell: T-A-B

Tab key The keyboard key that creates a specific, preset amount of space by moving the cursor forward one tab stop.

- Fingerspell: T-A-B

- **key** Push the extended thumb of the right *10 hand* downward a short distance in front of the right side of the body.

---

table In data processing, a way of organizing data or text in rows and columns.

- **chart** Bring the right *4 hand* from in front of the left shoulder, palm in and fingers pointing left.

---

talk Computer programs that are compatible are said to be able to *talk with* (or *to*) each other. See sign for CONVERSATIONAL.

---

tape A long strip of magnetic plastic, usually on a reel, for recording audio or visual signals.

- **tape** Beginning with both *T hands* in front of each side of the chest, palms forward, move the hands in simultaneous double circles.

---

target See sign for DESTINATION.

---

task Any operation that a computer performs.

- **work** Tap the heel of the right *S hand*, palm forward, with a double movement on the back of the left *S hand* held in front of the body, palm down.

---

taskbar In Windows, the bar at the bottom of the display screen, used for launching applications and switching between tasks that have been minimized.

- **work** Tap the heel of the right *S hand*, palm forward, with a double movement on the back of the left *S hand* held in front of the body, palm down.

- **bar** Move the fingers of the right *G hand*, palm forward, from left to right in front of the chest.

task switching Moving from one application to another.

- **work** Tap the heel of the right *S hand*, palm forward, with a double movement on the back of the left *S hand* held in front of the body, palm down.

- **exchange** Beginning with both *modified X hands* in front of the body, right hand somewhat forward of the left hand, move the right hand back toward the body in an upward arc while moving the left hand forward with a downward arc.

TCP/IP Initialism for *Transmission Control Protocol/Internet Protocol.* The standard procedure for sending data packets between unlike networks on the Internet.

- Fingerspell: T-C-P-I-P

technical See sign for TECHNOLOGY.

technology or **technical** The knowledge and methods used to create a product.

- **technology** Tap the bent middle finger of the right *5 hand*, palm up, upward on the little-finger side of the left *open hand* with a double movement.

telecommunications The transfer of data from one place to another over communications lines.

- **call** Bring the index finger of the right *X hand*, palm down, from the base off the fingertip of the extended left index finger held in front of the chest, palm right and finger pointing forward.

- **communication** Move both *C hands*, palms facing each other, forward and back from the mouth with an alternating movement.

telecommunications software Software that transforms a computer into a terminal capable of connecting to a multiuser computer system by means of the telephone.

- **call** Bring the index finger of the right *X hand*, palm down, from the base off the fingertip of the extended left index finger held in front of the chest, palm right and finger pointing forward.

- **communication** Move both *C hands*, palms facing each other, forward and back from the mouth with an alternating movement.

- Fingerspell: S-W

teletype See sign for TTY.

template A standard format used to create standardized documents. Same sign used for **boilerplate**.

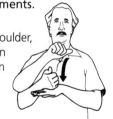

- **set-up** Beginning with the right *10 hand* in front of the right shoulder, palm down, twist the wrist up with a circular movement and then move the right hand straight down to land the little-finger side on the back of the left *open hand*, palm down.

- **copy**[1] Move the fingers of the right *curved hand* from touching the palm of the left *open hand* while closing the right fingers and thumb, forming a *flattened O hand*.

terminal

terminal or **monitor** A device for entering information into a central computer that includes a keyboard and display screen for viewing the information.

- **terminal** Beginning with the index-finger sides of both *T hands* together in front of the chest, palms forward, bring the hands apart to in front of each shoulder and then straight down.

---

test To ascertain that hardware or software is working properly by subjecting it to diagnostics.

- **test** With both extended index fingers pointing forward in front of the chest, palms down, bring the hands downward while bending the index fingers into *X hands* and continuing down while extending the index fingers again.

---

text Any combination of characters and symbols that conveys a message.

- **sentences** Beginning with the fingertips of both *F hands* touching in front of the chest, palms facing each other, pull the hands apart to in front of each side of the chest with a double movement.

---

text editor See sign for EDITOR.

---

text file A file having only characters and symbols without formatting. Text files often have the filename extension ".txt."

- **sentences** Beginning with the fingertips of both *F hands* touching in front of the chest, palms facing each other, pull the hands apart to in front of each side of the chest with a double movement.

- **file** Slide the little-finger side of the right *B hand*, palm angled up, between the fingers of the left *B hand*, palm facing in, first between the index and middle fingers and then between the middle and ring fingers.

---

throughput The amount of data transferred from one place to another or processed in a specified amount of time.

- **through** Slide the little-finger side of the right *open hand*, palm in and fingers angled to the left, between the middle finger and ring finger of the left *open hand* held in front of the chest, palm right and fingers pointing up.

---- [sign continues] -->

240

■ **put** Beginning with both *flattened O hands* in front of the body, palms facing down, move the hands forward in small arcs.

TIFF Acronym for *Tagged Image File Format.* A type of graphics file.

■ Fingerspell: T-I-F-F

time-sharing The apparently simultaneous use of a computer that is programmed to allocate its processing time either between several users or between programs.

■ **time** Tap the bent index finger of the right *X hand*, palm down, with a double movement on the wrist of the downturned left hand.

■ **share** Move the little-finger side of the right *open hand,* palm in, back and forth with a double movement at the base of the index finger of the left *open hand,* palm in.

time slice The amount of time allocated to an application by a computer when several programs are being run at the same time.

■ **time** Tap the bent index finger of the right *X hand*, palm down, with a double movement on the wrist of the downturned left hand.

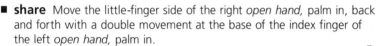

■ **slice** Bring the palm side of the right *open hand,* palm left and fingers pointing forward, from in front of the chest straight down near the thumb side of the left *S hand* held in front of the body, palm down.

title bar A thin horizontal bar across the top of a window that contains the name of the window, including the name of the open file, as well as the maximize, minimize, restore, and exit buttons.

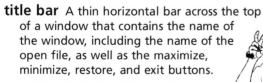

■ **title** Beginning with both *bent V hands* near each side of the head, palms facing forward, twist the hands while bending the fingers down, ending with the palms facing back.

---- [sign continues] ---->

- **bar** Move the fingers of the right *G hand*, palm forward, from left to right in front of the chest.

toggle, DIP switch, or **flip-flop** An option for a command or program that can be turned either off or on.

- **toggle** With the palm sides of both *L hands* together in front of the chest, palms facing each other, flip the hands over, exchanging places.

token In programming languages, a single character, symbol, or keyword. See sign for KEYWORD.

toner An electrically charged dry, powdery ink used by copy machines and laser printers.

- Fingerspell: T-O-N-E-R

toolbar See signs for BAR[1,2].

toolbox A set of programs with icons and buttons that help programmers develop software without having to create individual routines from scratch.

- Fingerspell: T-O-O-L

- **box** Beginning with both *open hands* in front of each side of the chest, palms facing each other and fingers pointing forward, move the hands deliberately in opposite directions, ending with the left hand near the chest and the right hand several inches forward of the left hand, both palms facing in.

top-down In programming, writing programs in separate pieces beginning with the larger parts first and then filling in the details later.

- **top-down** Bring the extended right index finger, palm forward and finger pointing up, upward to touch the palm of the left *open hand* held in front of the chest, palm down and fingers pointing right. Then turn the right hand to point the index finger down and move the hand down again.

touchpad An input device, used especially on a portable computer instead of a mouse, consisting of a layer of soft plastic covering keys or buttons that send signals to the computer when touched or that is sensitive to a sliding finger used to move the pointer on-screen.

- **square** Beginning with both extended index fingers touching in front of the chest, palms facing forward, move the hands outward to each side of the chest and then down and back together in front of the chest.

- **touch** Bring the bent middle finger of the right hand, palm down, downward to touch the back of the left *open hand* held in front of the body, palm down.

---

track A circular path on the surface of a recording medium, as a disk or tape, along which electronic data can be recorded.

- **disk** Move the fingertips of the right *D hand,* palm facing down and index finger pointing forward, in a double circle on the upturned left *open hand.*

- **track** Move the extended right index finger, palm in and finger pointing down, in a repeated flat circle over the left *open hand* held in front of the body, palm up.

---

trackball An input device with a ball on top that is rotated with the fingers and that operates similarly to a mouse.

- **trackball** Move the right *open hand*, palm down, in a flat circle in front of the right side of the body.

---

transient Not permanent; lasting for a short time. Compare RESIDENT PROGRAM.

- **pop-up + disappear** Insert the extended right index finger, palm forward and finger pointing up, upward between the middle finger and ring finger of the left hand held across the chest, palm down and fingers pointing right. Then pull the right hand down again.

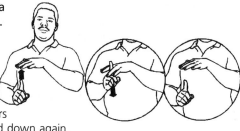

Transmission Control Protocol/Internet Protocol

Transmission Control Protocol/Internet Protocol See sign for TCP/IP.

trapping See sign for INTERRUPT.

tree structure See sign for NODE².

triple-click To click the mouse button three times in rapid succession in order to access features.

- **three** Hold up the right *3 hand*, palm forward, in front of the right shoulder.

- **click** Beginning with the right index finger pointing forward in front of the chest, bend the finger deliberately downward.

troubleshoot To locate an error through a process of elimination.

- **analyze** With both *V hands* pointing toward each other in front of the chest, palms down, move the fingers down and apart with a double movement, bending the fingers each time.

- **problem** Beginning with the knuckles of both *bent V hands*, touching in front of the chest, twist the hands in opposite directions with a deliberate movement, rubbing the knuckles against each other.

truncate or **cut off** To shorten by cutting off a part. For example, cutting text to fit the space allotted in a database field.

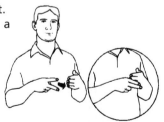

- **truncate** Move the right *V hand*, palm left, forward across the fingertips of the left *open hand*, palm in and fingers pointing right, with a deliberate movement while closing the fingers of the *V hand* together.

TTY Abbreviation for *teletype*. A dumb terminal consisting of a keyboard and monitor that enables information to be sent and received from another computer.

- Fingerspell: T-T-Y

turnkey system A packaged computer system complete with computer and software, as well as monitor, keyboard, disk drives, and other peripherals.

■ **include** Swing the right *5 hand*, palm down, in a circular movement over the left *O hand*, palm in, while changing into a *flattened O hand*, ending with the fingertips of the right hand inserted in the center of the thumb side of the left hand.

■ **program** Move the middle finger of the right *P hand*, palm left, from the fingertips to the base of the left *open hand*, palm right and fingers pointing up. Repeat the movement on the back side of the left hand.

tutorial An on-screen training session that guides a user through a procedure, often interactively.

■ **tutor** Beginning with both *T hands* in front of each side of the head, palms facing each other, move the hands forward with a short double movement.

■ **person marker** Move both *open hands*, palms facing each other, downward along each side of the body.

tweak To change settings on hardware or software so it more nearly suits the user's needs.

■ **little-bit** Beginning with the left *6 hand* in front of the right side of the chest, palm up, flick the thumb off the little finger with a quick movement.

■ **change**[2] With the palm side of both *A hands* facing each other, twist the wrists in opposite directions in order to reverse positions.

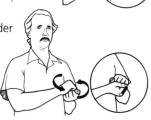

TXT

TXT The file extension (.txt) identifying text files.
- Fingerspell: T-X-T

type To enter characters by pressing keys on the keyboard.
- **type** Beginning with both *5 hands* in front of the body, palms down and fingers pointing forward, wiggle the fingers with alternating movements.

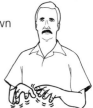

typeface The design of characters in a type font.
- **type** Beginning with both *5 hands* in front of the body, palms down and fingers pointing forward, wiggle the fingers with alternating movements.

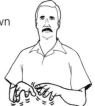

- **shape** Bring both *10 hands*, palms facing forward, downward with a wavy movement from in front of the chest to in front of each side of the waist.

typewriter A machine used for writing characters mechanically, usually directly on paper, by manually pressing the keys on a keyboard.
- **typewriter** Beginning with both *curved 5 hands* in front of the body, palms facing down, move the hands up and down with a short alternating double movement.

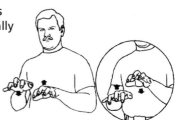

undelete A utility or command that can often recover deleted files. See sign for RECOVER.

---

underline or **underscore** In word processing, a type attribute that produces a line under other characters in the text.

- **under** Move the right *10 hand*, palm left, from in front of the chest downward and forward under the left *open hand* held in front of the chest, palm down and fingers pointing right.

- **line** Beginning with the extended little fingers of both *I hands* touching in front of the chest, palms facing in, move both hands outward.

---

underscore See sign for UNDERLINE.

---

undo A command that cancels the effects of the most recent keyboard action and puts the text back the way it was.

- Fingerspell: U-N-D-O

UnErase A program or utility developed by Peter Norton in the 1980s that can often recover deleted files. See sign for RECOVER.

Uniform Resource Locator See sign for URL.

---

universal language or **common language** A computer programming language that is understood by two or more computers with different machine languages, such as BASIC, Pascal, FORTRAN, and COBOL.

- **share** Move the little-finger side of the right *open hand*, palm in, back and forth with a double movement at the base of the index finger of the left *open hand*, palm in.

- **language** Beginning with the thumbs of both *L hands* near each other in front of the chest, palms angled down, bring the hands outward with a wavy movement to in front of each side of the chest.

universal product code

universal product code See sign for BAR CODE.

universal serial bus See sign for USB.

UNIX An easy-to-use, powerful operating system capable of running a number of jobs at once and used on a variety of computers from mainframes to micro-computers.
- Fingerspell: U-N-I-X

unpack To separate short units of data that have been previously packed. Compare PACK.
- **box** Beginning with both *open hands* in front of each side of the chest, palms facing each other and fingers pointing forward, move the hands deliberately in opposite directions, ending with the left hand near the chest and the right hand several inches forward of the left hand, both palms facing in.

- **throw-out** Beginning with both *S hands* in front of the body, right palm up and left palm down, move the hands quickly upward to the right while opening into *5 hands*.

up (of a computer) Operating correctly and available for use. Compare DOWN. See sign for EXECUTE.

update To make files more current by adding new or revised data.
- **update** Beginning with the right *10 hand* in front of the right side of the chest, palm down, and the left *10 hand* in front of the left side of the chest, palm right, twist the right wrist to the right to turn the palm left. Then bring the knuckles of the right hand against the heel of the left hand, pushing it forward.

upgrade To install a newer, revised version of a program, usually to improve function or add features.
- **improve** Touch the little-finger side of the right *open hand*, palm back and fingers pointing left, first to the wrist, then to the forearm, and then to the upper bent left arm.

upload or **export** To transmit a file from your computer to another computer. Compare DOWNLOAD.

- **upload** Beginning with both *bent V hands*, palms facing each other in front of the body, move the hands in toward the chest and then upward to the right while straightening the fingers forming *V hands*.

uppercase[1] or **caps** A typographic style in which all letters, or sometimes the first letters of a group of words, are capitalized. Compare LOWERCASE.

- **capital** Hold the right *modified C hand*, palm forward, in front of the right side of the body.

uppercase[2] or **caps** (alternate sign)

- **capital** Hold the right *modified C hand*, palm forward, in front of the right side of the body.

- **letter** Touch the extended thumb of the right *10 hand* to the lips, palm in, and then move the thumb downward to touch the thumb of the left *10 hand* held in front of the chest, palm in.

uptime[1] The time that the computer is running and functioning. Compare DOWNTIME.

- **up**[2] Move the extended thumb of the right *10 hand*, palm left and thumb pointing up, upward a short distance in front of the right side of the body.

- **time** Tap the bent index finger of the right *X hand*, palm down, with a double movement on the wrist of the downturned left hand.

uptime² (alternate sign)

- ■ **use** Beginning with the heel of the right *U hand* on the back of the left *S hand*, move the right hand in a small upward circle.

- ■ **time** Tap the bent index finger of the right *X hand*, palm down, with a double movement on the wrist of the downturned left hand.

URL Initialism for *Uniform Resource Locator*. A kind of command used on the Internet to locate types of information. URLs include the protocol, like *http*, *ftp*, or *news*, and the IP address and/or domain name. An example would be *http://www.blankuniversity.edu*.

- ■ Fingerspell: U-R-L

USB Initialism for *universal serial bus*. A new serial port standard that allows up to 127 different devices to be connected to a single port.

- ■ Fingerspell: U-S-B

user A person using a computer and software as a tool.

- ■ **use** Beginning with the heel of the right *U hand* on the back of the left *S hand*, move the right hand in a small upward circle.

- ■ **person marker** Move both *open hands*, palms facing each other, downward along the sides of the body.

user-friendly¹ or **intuitive** Referring to hardware or software that is easy to use, especially for novice computer users and often without referring to a manual.

- ■ **use** Beginning with the heel of the right *U hand* on the back of the left *S hand*, move the right hand in a small upward circle.

---- [sign continues] -->

- **easy** Brush the fingertips of the right *open hand* upward on the back of the fingertips of the left *curved hand* with a double movement, both palms up.

user-friendly[2] or **intuitive** (alternate sign)

- **use** Beginning with the heel of the right *U hand* on the back of the left *S hand*, move the right hand in a small upward circle.

- **person marker** Move both *open hands*, palms facing each other, downward along the sides of the body.

- **friendly** With both *5 hands* near the cheeks, palms facing back, wiggle the fingers.

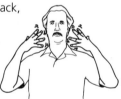

user ID or **user name** A number or code word used to identify the person using the computer on a multi-user computer or network. Unlike a password, the user ID is not normally secret.

- **use** Beginning with the heel of the right *U hand* on the back of the left *S hand*, move the right hand in a small upward circle.

- **person marker** Move both *open hands*, palms facing each other, downward along the sides of the body.

- Fingerspell: I-D

user interface The part of the system's software that communicates with the user. The user interface may use commands or menus or, what is now common on personal computers, a graphical interface with windows and icons.

- **use** Beginning with the heel of the right *U hand* on the back of the left *S hand*, move the right hand in a small upward circle.

- **person marker** Move both *open hands*, palms facing each other, downward along the sides of the body.

- **interface** Beginning with both *5 hands* in front of each side of the chest, fingers angled toward each other, push the hands toward each other, causing the fingers to mesh together.

---

user manual See sign for MANUAL

---

user name See sign for USER ID.

---

utility or **software tools** A program that assists the user in maintaining or improving the efficiency of a computer system.

- **serve** Beginning with both *open hands* in front of each side of the body, palms facing up and right hand closer to the body than the left, move the hands forward and back with an alternating movement.

validation The examination of data for correctness as measured against certain criteria such as format, ranges, etc. Compare VERIFICATION. Related form: **validate**.

- **right**[3] With the index fingers of both hands extended forward at right angles, palms angled in and right hand above left, bring the little-finger side of the right hand sharply down across the thumb side of the left hand.

value In databases or spreadsheets, a number entered into a cell.

- **value** Beginning with the index fingers of both *V hands* touching in front of the chest, palms facing down, move the hands outward and upward in arcs, ending with the index fingers touching and the palms facing forward.

variable[1] In programming, a symbol that represents a numeric value or string of text that changes during processing.

- **variable** Beginning with both *V hands* in front of the chest, palms down and fingers pointing forward, move the hands apart in a large wavy movement to in front of each shoulder.

variable[2] (alternate sign)

- **vary** Beginning with both extended index fingers pointing forward in front of the chest, palms facing down, move the right hand up and the left hand down with an alternating repeated movement as the hands move outward.

VBA See sign for VISUAL BASIC FOR APPLICATION.

VBScript See sign for VISUAL BASIC FOR APPLICATION.

verification To check data so as to determine whether a data processing operation has been accomplished accurately. Compare VALIDATION. See sign for VERIFY.

253

verify, check, or **proof** To determine whether a data processing operation has been accomplished accurately, such as to check data validity. Same sign used for **verification**.

- **verify** Move the index finger of the right *V hand*, palm forward, from near the right eye down to strike the palm of the left *open hand* held in front of the chest.

---

version A specific release of a software product, usually numbered in ascending order.

- Fingerspell: V-E-R

video A visual display.

- **video** With the thumb of the right *5 hand*, palm forward, against the palm of the left *open hand*, palm right and fingers pointing up, wiggle the right fingers.

---

video adapter See signs for GRAPHICS ADAPTER CARD[1,2].

---

video card See signs for GRAPHICS ADAPTER CARD[1,2].

---

videoconferencing Transmitting video signals as well as telephone and computer data signals so users in remote locations can communicate both visually and auditorily.

- **video** With the thumb of the right *5 hand*, palm forward, against the palm of the left *open hand*, palm right and fingers pointing up, wiggle the right fingers.

- **meeting** Beginning with the thumbs of both *5 hands* near each other in front of the chest, close the fingers to the thumbs with a double movement, forming *flattened O hands* each time.

---

video digitizer A device that converts the signal from a video camera into digital form for computer storage and use.

- **video** With the thumb of the right *5 hand*, palm forward, against the palm of the left *open hand*, palm right and fingers pointing up, wiggle the right fingers.

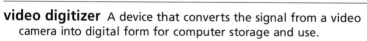

---- [sign continues] --->

- **convert**[1] With both *C hands* in front of the chest, thumbs touching, turn the right hand down and back again.

- **person marker** Move both *open hands*, palms facing each other, downward along the sides of the body.

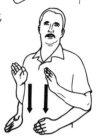

view The presentation of the contents of a database in different ways.

- **perspective** Beginning with the index finger of both *V hands* near each side of the face, palms down and fingers pointing toward each other, bring the hands outward in an arc and then forward toward each other in front of the chest.

virtual[1] Simulated by computer software to appear to be, rather than *actually* being. You can have a virtual hard disk in RAM, for example, or virtual RAM on your hard disk. Compare LOGICAL, PHYSICAL.

- **fake** Beginning with the index finger of the right *4 hand* touching the right side of the forehead, move the hand forward in several short movements.

virtual[2] (alternate sign)

- **virtual** Beginning with the index-finger side of the right *V hand* touching the right side of the forehead, palm left, move the hand forward in a double arc.

virtual memory or **virtual storage** A kind of imaginary memory created by a technique for managing limited RAM by swapping segments of the program and data from a lower-speed storage, usually a disk, in segments called a *page*. The lower-speed storage is called virtual memory.

- **fake** Beginning with the index finger of the right *4 hand* touching the right side of the forehead, move the hand forward in several short movements.

---- [sign continues] ---->

virtual memory

■ **memory** Beginning with the fingertips of the right *curved hand* touching the right side of the forehead, palm down, bring the hand forward and down while closing the fingers into an *S hand*, palm in.

virtual reality or **VR** A computer technology that immerses the user in the illusion of a computer-generated world.

■ **fake** Beginning with the index finger of the right *4 hand* touching the right side of the forehead, move the hand forward in several short movements.

■ **real** Move the side of the extended right index finger from in front of the mouth, palm left and finger pointing up, upward and forward in an arc.

virtual storage See sign for VIRTUAL MEMORY.

virus Self-replicating code planted in a program, containing unauthorized and unwanted instructions that disrupt a computer's normal operation; often acquired from downloaded software, pirated software, or an e-mail attachment from an unknown source.

■ Fingerspell: V-I-R-U-S

Visual Basic for Application, VBA, or **VBScript** A form of BASIC that permits the user to create programs using BASIC commands through a graphical environment, including dragging and dropping, to modify the on-screen interface, as in Excel, Word, and Access.

■ Fingerspell: V-B

■ **script** Move the right *S hand*, palm left, downward across the palm of the left *5 hand* held in front of the chest, palm right and fingers angled forward.

vocabulary The collection of words that are acceptable for use in a particular programming language.

■ **vocabulary** Tap the fingertips of the right *V hand*, palm down, with a double movement on the extended left index finger held in front of the body, palm in and finger pointing right.

voice input See sign for VOICE RECOGNITION.

voice mail A type of e-mail in which voice messages spoken into a telephone are stored in a computer as digital data and converted back to voice when recalled.

- **voice** Move the fingertips of the right *V hand*, palm down, upward on the throat with a double movement.

- **letter** Touch the extended thumb of the right *10 hand* to the lips, palm in, and then move the thumb downward to touch the thumb of the left *10 hand* held in front of the chest, palm in.

voice recognition, speech recognition, voice input, Voice User Interface, or **VUI** An interface that causes the computer to accept and act on voice commands.

- **voice** Move the fingertips of the right *V hand*, palm down, upward on the throat with a double movement.

- **recognize** Bring the extended curved right index finger from touching the cheek near the right eye, palm left, downward to touch the palm of the left *open hand*, palm right in front of the chest.

Voice User Interface See sign for VOICE RECOGNITION.

volume See signs for DISK[1,2].

volume label The name assigned to a hard disk, floppy disk, or other storage medium to identify it.

- **disk** Move the fingertips of the right *D hand*, palm facing down and index finger pointing forward, in a double circle on the upturned left *open hand*.

---- [sign continues] ---➔

volume label

■ **name** Tap the middle-finger side of the right *H hand* across the index-finger side of the left *H hand* with a double movement.

VR See sign for VIRTUAL REALITY.

VUI Initialism for *Voice User Interface.* See sign for VOICE RECOGNITION.

wait state The short delay that occurs when the microprocessor accesses data from memory. Compare ZERO WAIT STATE.

- **wait** Beginning with both *curved 5 hands* in front of the body, palms facing up, wiggle the fingers with a repeated movement.

- **time** Tap the bent index finger of the right *X hand*, palm down, with a double movement on the wrist of the downturned left hand.

walk-through A review session in which a phase of system or program development is reviewed by peers to identify errors.

- **walk** Beginning with both *open hands* in front of the body, right palm in and fingers pointing down, left palm down and fingers pointing forward, swing the fingers of both hands upward and downward with an alternating movement by bending the wrists.

- **through** Slide the little-finger side of the right *open hand*, palm in and fingers angled to the left, between the middle finger and ring finger of the left *open hand* held in front of the chest, palm right and fingers pointing up.

WAN Acronym for *wide area network*. A network of computers that spans a large distance, as opposed to a local area network. Compare LAN.

- Fingerspell: W-A-N

warm boot[1], **reboot,** or **reset** The process of restarting a computer without turning off the power, usually by pressing a "restart" button.

- **warm** Beginning with the fingers of the right *E hand* near the mouth, palm in, move the hand forward in a small arc while opening the fingers into a *C hand*, ending with the palm up.

---- [sign continues] --→

warm boot

- **kick** Bring the right *B hand* upward to strike the index-finger side of the right hand against the little-finger side of the left *open hand* held in front of the chest, palm angled up and fingers pointing forward.

warm boot², reboot, or reset (alternate sign)

- **start** Beginning with the extended right index finger, palm down, inserted between the index and middle fingers of the left *open hand*, palm right and fingers pointing forward, twist the right hand back, ending with palm in.

- **again** Bring the fingertips of the right *bent hand* against the palm of the left *open hand* held in front of the chest.

warm boot³ reboot, or reset (alternate sign)

- **enter** Move the back of the right *open hand* forward in a downward arc under the palm of the left *open hand*, both palms down.

- **again** Bring the fingertips of the right *bent hand* against the palm of the left *open hand* held in front of the chest.

Web¹ Short for *World Wide Web*. The group of connected servers that allow users to access information on the Internet using formatted text and graphics.
- Fingerspell: W-E-B

Web² (alternate sign)
- Fingerspell: W-W-W

Web browser or **browser** The software that enables a user to retrieve documents written in HTML or XML from the Web, jump to links specified in retrieved documents, and save and print the retrieved documents.

- Fingerspell: W-E-B
- **search** Move the right *C hand*, palm left, with a double circular movement in front of the face.

- **person marker** Move both *open hands*, palms facing each other, downward along the sides of the body.

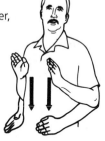

Web catalog See sign for SEARCH ENGINE.

Webmaster A person responsible for the visual layout of a Web site, its written content, and its links to other sites, as well as related processes that enable the Webmaster to follow up on users' inquiries.

- Fingerspell: W-E-B
- **boss** Tap the fingertips of the right *curved 5 hand* on the right shoulder with a repeated movement.

Web page A document that may include text, graphics, sound, video, etc., created to be shared by others who visit it on the Web.

- Fingerspell: W-E-B
- **page** Strike the extended thumb of the right *10 hand*, palm down, against the left open palm with a double upward movement.

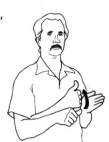

Web site A group of related Web pages.

- Fingerspell: W-E-B
- **set-up** Beginning with the right *10 hand* in front of the right shoulder, palm down, twist the wrist up with a circular movement and then move the right hand down to land the little-finger side on the back of the left *open hand*, palm down.

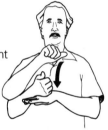

---- [sign continues] ---->

Web site

- **area** Beginning with the thumbs of both *A hands* touching in front of the chest, palms facing down, move the hands apart in a backward circular movement until they touch again near the chest.

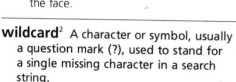

wide area network See sign for WAN.

wildcard[1] A character or symbol (*) used in place of a number of possible combinations when you search for text and don't know the spelling or the whole name. Same sign used for **asterisk**.

- **star** Brush the sides of both extended index fingers against each other, palms facing forward, with an alternating movement as the hands move upward in front of the face.

wildcard[2] A character or symbol, usually a question mark (?), used to stand for a single missing character in a search string.

- **question** Move the extended right index finger from pointing forward in front of the right shoulder, palm facing down, downward with a curving movement while retracting the index finger and then pointing it straight forward again at the bottom of the curve.

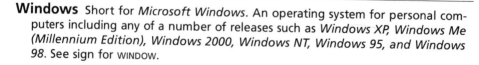

window An area having data, programs, or information on the display screen. A window can be moved, resized, opened, and closed, so that a user can switch between several open windows. Same sign used for **Windows**.

- **window** Beginning with the little-finger side of the right *B hand* on the index-finger side of the left *B hand*, both palms facing in and fingers pointing in opposite directions, move the right hand up and the left hand down simultaneously.

Windows Short for *Microsoft Windows*. An operating system for personal computers including any of a number of releases such as *Windows XP, Windows Me (Millennium Edition), Windows 2000, Windows NT, Windows 95,* and *Windows 98*. See sign for WINDOW.

wizard 1. A computer user who can solve most problems in most cases without assistance of any kind. 2. A software utility that enables the user to perform an essential task, such as installing an application with appropriate settings.

- Fingerspell: W-I-Z

word A collection of data bits processed as a unit.

- **word** Touch the extended fingers of the right *G hand*, palm left, against the extended left index finger pointing up in front of the chest, palm right.

word processing A type of program that transforms the computer into a tool for creating, editing, proofreading, formatting, and printing documents.

- **word** Touch the extended fingers of the right *G hand*, palm left, against the extended left index finger pointing up in front of the chest, palm right.

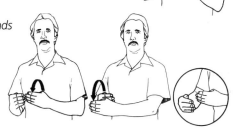

- **process** Beginning with both *open hands* in front of the body, palms facing in, left fingers pointing right and right fingers pointing left, and the left hand closer to the chest than the right hand, move the left over the right hand and then the right over the left hand in an alternating movement.

word wrap A word processing feature that automatically moves words down to the beginning of the next line if they extend beyond the right margin.

- **sentence** Beginning with the fingertips of both *F hands* touching in front of the chest, palms facing each other, pull the hands apart to in front of each side of the chest.

- **wrap** Beginning with the fingers of both *F hands* touching in front of the chest, palms facing each other, move the right hand quickly down under the left hand.

work area The area on a display screen on which you build a spreadsheet.

- **screen** Beginning with both extended index fingers side by side in front of the chest, palms facing down and fingers pointing forward, bring the hands apart to in front of each shoulder, then straight down, and finally back together again in front of the lower chest.

---- [sign continues] --->

work area

- **work** Tap the heel of the right *S hand*, palm forward, with a double movement on the back of the left *S hand* held in front of the body, palm down.

- **area** Beginning with the thumbs of both *A hands* touching in front of the chest, palms facing down, move the hands apart in a backward circular movement until they touch again near the chest.

workstation The configuration of computer equipment designed for use by one person at a time, including hardware and software.

- **work** Tap the heel of the right *S hand*, palm forward, with a double movement on the back of the left *S hand* held in front of the body, palm down.

- **walls** Beginning with the *B hands* in front of each shoulder, palms facing each other and fingers angled up, bring the hands straight downward while turning the fingers forward.

World Wide Web See signs for WEB[1,2].

WPD A file extension used for a word processing file.

- Fingerspell: W-P-D

write 1. To be the author of. 2. To record on disk. Same sign used for **code**.

- **write** Move the fingers of the right *modified X hand*, palm left, with a wiggly movement from the heel to the fingers of the left *open hand* held in front of the body.

write-protect To mark a disk or tape, physically or through software, so as to keep it from being written to.

- **write** Move the fingers of the right *modified X hand*, palm left, with a wiggly movement from the heel to the fingers of the left *open hand* held in front of the body.

---- [sign continues] --→

264

■ **protect** With the wrists of both *S hands* crossed in front of the chest, palms facing in opposite directions, move the hands forward with a short double movement.

XLS A file extension used for a spreadsheet file.

- Fingerspell: X-L-S

XML Initialism for *Extensible Markup Language*. A language used to create a markup scheme for tagging the elements of an electronic document according to their content. The document can then be produced in different media formats by applying external style sheets and transmitted, with hypertext links to other documents; increasingly used on the Web instead of HTML. XML is a simplified form of SGML.

- Fingerspell: X-M-L

zap (*Slang*) To permanently delete a file or clear a screen accidentally. See sign for DELETE.

---

zero wait state A condition in which the microprocessor does not have to wait until it can read information from RAM.

- ■ **none** Move both *flattened O hands* from in front of the chest downward and outward to each side.

- ■ **wait** Beginning with both *curved 5 hands* in front of the body, palms facing up, wiggle the fingers with a repeated movement.

ZIP A file extension used to identify files that have been compressed with the PKZIP utility, and which must be uncompressed with the PKUNZIP utility or similar software.

- ■ Fingerspell: Z-I-P

ZIP disk A removable cartridge that can hold more data than a typical floppy disk.

- ■ Fingerspell: Z-I-P
- ■ **disk** Move the fingertips of the right *D hand,* palm facing down and index finger pointing forward, in a double circle on the upturned left *open hand.*

American Manual Alphabet

A, a   B, b   C, c   D, d   E, e   F, f   G, g   H, h

I, i   J, j   K, k   L, l   M, m   N, n   O, o

P, p   Q, q   R, r   S, s   T, t   U, u   V, v   W, w

X, x   Y, y   Z, z

Handshapes

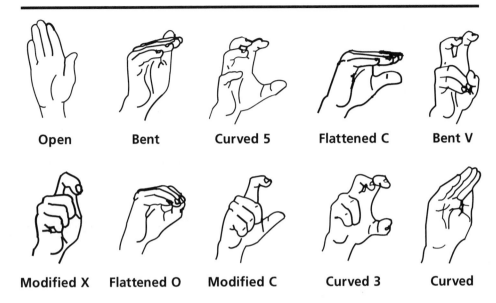

Open   Bent   Curved 5   Flattened C   Bent V

Modified X   Flattened O   Modified C   Curved 3   Curved

Numbers

One, 1   Two, 2   Three, 3   Four, 4   Five, 5

Six, 6   Seven, 7   Eight, 8   Nine, 9   Ten, 10